ESSENTIAL GRANTS MANAGEMENT DOCUMENTS

By Marricke Kofi GANE

ESSENTIAL GRANTS MANAGEMENT DOCUMENTS

By Marricke Kofi Gane

ISBN: 978-1-909326-25-5

Published by:
MarrickeGane Publishing

Distributed by:
Amazon

Contents

INTRODUCTION

I consider myself very fortunate to have not only worked as a finance professional in the International Development sector but more interestingly, on either side of the sector's divide – first as grant and funding recipient and then, subsequently in a donor capacity, awarding grants to organisations worldwide.

The documents listed in this book are a few I have used over the years and found very useful for grants financial management whether as a Grant recipient or as a Donor. What I have done is to take what has worked in practice and evolved them into tools more easily applicable in a wider scope of Grants management scenarios.

That's exactly why it was published – to make available to others in the development sector, relevant and well-tested documentations to help in their financial management of grant funding contracts whether as grant-makers or grant recipients.

The general idea is that these documents will guide your thinking on similar documents you wish to use in your organisation. It can also be copied for immediate use. Besides this provision, others may wish to have a PDF version of the standalone documents downloaded for conversion, editing and use – if this is so, you will be glad to know you can find single, PDF downloadable versions of these documents on my website www.grants-consultant.com

1.

AUDITOR SELECTION GUIDELINES
(FOR FIELD OFFICE OR PROJECT AUDITS)

INTRODUCTION

This document is a guidance, to help in selecting a professional firm or person(s) to carry out an audit of one kind or the other of (i) A development organisation (ii) a field office and/or (iii) a development project. It can be used on its own, or as a supplement to the user's own internal guidance. I suggest that a full service proposal (technical and financial) should still be requested from the potential auditor as part o fthe assessment process.

The xx main weighted criteria applied in this document to determine the suitablity of an audit firm (also includes a person) are as follows:

(1) **The firms qualities:** This requires an assessment of the firm's size, local and international affiliations, its staff and the qualifications of both the firm and its staff. The size of a firm does not necessarily imply it can deliver value for money and as such, it is essential that the quality of the firm is looked at holistically and not just from its physical appeal. A firm with international affiliations could also mean that the standards of its operations is likely to be comparable *(at least to some extent)* with other internationally known firms of good repute *(normally, for an international firm to award its affiliation to a local firm, it would have assessed its practices, to ensure that they meet a certain minmum quality)*

(2) **Clients and Previous Experience:** This requires an assessment of the Auditor's (firm or person) experience with other clients in the same industry as yours or, of similar projects carried out by your organisation: e.g. firm "A" who's audit experience includes 2 manufacturing companies and 2 large distilleries will not have have the same industyr focused experience as firm "B" whose experiences include the audits of 1 DFID funded project, 1 USAID funded project, 1 local country office of Amnesty International and 1 local manufacturing company. Where you deem it necessary, you could ask the audit firm(s) to provide you with a list of referees of other organisations that bear some similarites with yours or your projects in order to obtain references from.

(3) **The Methodology & Task Understanding:** Here, you will need to assess the methods of auditing highlighted by the firm as well as their understanding o fthe task in hand. The two go hand-in-hand as a misunderstanding of the assign-

ment you want carried out will automatically be reflected in the wrong selection of applicable methodologies. You must insist that the proposal presented by the firm, includes a paragraph that states very clearly, its understanding of the audit engagement. Assessing the firm's methodology however can be a little tricky for persons with no prior audit recruitment experience but a few things are worth noting:

(i)   it is essential that the methodology outlined by the auditor should be the closest to satisfying the audit objectives: e.g. if the purpose of the audit was to investigate a sizeable fraud in a local office's asset purchases, the audit methodology should score very low if it suggested a sample testing of about 5-7% of the asset acquisition transactions.

(ii) the methodology outlined by the audit firm should match the prameters of the project or organisation being audited: e.g. if the audit is to cover a project in a very remote area with very basic, manual records, it will be incompatible for a substantial part of the auditor's methodology to be centered around, testing the project's IT systems

(iii) There must also be a balance between an audit of the internal controls that exists within the project or local office and the detailed testing of the actual transactions generated by such control environments. Some firms may be tempted to simply assess the control systems and control environmnets alone, to the detriment of an actual test, on the transactions generated, so there does need to be a good balance.

(4) **Time Allocation and Fees:** How much time is the auditor intending to spend on auditing your project, is an important consideration. But it doesn't end there. It is essential to also know the various categories of staff (and their experiences) to be employed on the process and how much time each will spend on the audit. It is essential, you get assurance that the list of staff provided will not be drastically changed – it is not unusual for some firms, to present personnel with excellent experiences as part of the proposed team and to substitute them for lower quality staff once the contract for audit is won. Also consider the reasonableness of the time proposed for the audit – if it is too low or too high, question it. Finally, be sure to ask the audit fee section to clarify if the fee

quoted is a wholesome fee, or if there are other "out-of-pocket" expenses to be paid by you, what they are and how much they cost.

PREPARING A REQUEST FOR AUDIT PROPOSAL

In putting together a Request for Proposals (RFP) for a new audit firm for your local office or specific project, the following considerations have to be made in order that the RFP process delivers the best impact:

- Provide a good background information on the project or office to be audited, its affiliations, staffing, supporting donors, specific grant conditions (where necessary, you may even include components of the grant agreement relevant to reporting and or audits
- Ensure that the RFP is clearly and concisely written
- Clearly state the scope of the work requested from the auditor i.e. the length and breadth of areas expected to be covered
- Challenge firms to demonstrate an understanding of the issues faced by your organization or project and for that matter, the scope of work highlighted
- Request specific information that has a direct bearing on bidding firms' ability to perform the work
- Allow for flexibility in the presentation of material rather than specifying particular formats for their presentation as this may tend to limit some otherwise vital information
- Indicate if and when (or whether at all) oral presentations are to be scheduled and when firms may expect to be notified of their participation.
- Be clear on what the decision process is likely to be like, including the ground rules, timing, communication of results, etc
- State whether or not site visits are expected to be part of the audits, the areas to be covered, any restrictions or preacutionary considerations in reaching those areas etc
- Provide a reasonable length of time within which the audit firms can prepare their proposal

SOME SPECIFIC QUESTIONS TO ASK POTENTIAL AUDITORS

FIRM OVERVIEW

1. Provide an overview of your audit firm, including details of your local and international qualifications, affiliations, staff size, scope of services, awards, memberships etc

2. Are there any legal actions or potential conflicts of interest relating to the firm that may impact the ability of the firm to provide us audit services?

3. When was the firm last subject to an independent quality assurance review and what was the nature of that review?

4. Is the firm in "good standing" with the national accounting regulatory body?

5. If the firm has international affiliation(s), what is (are) the nature(s) of such affiliation(s)?

ENGAGEMENT TEAM

1. Identify the partners, managers, seniors and trainees who will be deployed for our audit engagement, how they will be organized and what their levels of involvement will be.

2. Describe the roles and responsibilities of the individuals or positions listed above on this assignement

3. Provide resumes (CVs) showing their relevant development industry or project audit experiences

4. Describe what your engagement team's working relationship with our staff will be.

5. Identify other specialists who will participate on the assignment whether regularly or not

ASSIGNMENT MANAGEMENT

1. Describe how the firm will manage the assignment in order for the highest efficiency stating clearly how you will manage the collaboration of your staff with ours.

2. What is your firm's policy on staff replacement, substitutions and partner rotations? What arrangements does the firm have to ensure if key personnel on assignment become unavailable, they are substituted similarly qualified and experienced staff?

3. Assuming we already have an audit firm we no longer wish to employ, describe your firm's approach for a transitioning.

4. Provide a tentative timetable for the assignment, clearly indicating time allocated to work in our offices, field visits (where deemed necessary), quality assurance reviews by your firms internal mechanisms etc.

5. What is the firm's reporting approach as they relate to interim as well as final phases of the audit?

6. What is the firm's internal quality control and assurance procedures for specific audit assignments?

INDUSTRY EXPERIENCE

1. Describe your firm's relevant experience in the international development and donor related industry

2. Provide a list of 3-6 present or past clients of you firm in the international development and donor related industry stating the year in which you last dealt with each, and whether you are happy to put them forward as your referee

3. Having had experience of the international development sector, please state two areas your firm percieves are high risk areas for fraud or financial misappropriation

4. Having had experience of the international development sector, please state two new developments or trends in our sector, that your firm considers worth bearing in mind during this audit assignment

5. What is the firm's understanding of specific national statutory requirements that is likely to impact on the audit?

METHODOLOGY (YOU WAY OF AUDITING)

1. Outline the principal features of your audit plan - audit scope, planning, audit procedures, timetable, and other matters.

2. Describe your firm's use of advanced audit-related technologies.

3. Discuss your firm's process(es) for resolving issues. Who makes the final technical

4. decisions on controversial or emerging issues?

5. Describe how your firm's audit approach will yield value-added rewards to us

6. What is the firm's approach to reviewing any computerized and/or manual controls over the financial reporting system, including review of the financial system?

FEES AND OTHER EXPENSES

1. Provide estimated fixed-fee for the audit engagement indicating what services are included in these fees and what services are excluded.

2. Describe very clearly, what other out of pocket expenses will be charged on this assignment giving an estimation of what they cover and the rates to be charged. Please state which charges are contingent on certain occurences and what those trigger occurrences are.

3. Describe how the fee will be adjusted for additions or deletions of full or partial audit scopes or services no longer required or required to be added as the need may be.

4. For how many years can the proposed fee(s) be kept at the same level?

5. What would be the basis for fee increases in subsequent years?

JUSTIFICATION

Please summarize 5 main reasons our organisation would benefit from selecting and awarding your firm, this audit assignment

AUDIT FIRM SELECTION SCORE-SHEET

Introduction: The use of this scoring sheet is to help provide some structure, to the process of selecting an appropriate audit firm, using scores. The selection should generally be among the top 3 highest scoring firms. The scoring should be done by at least 3 persons and the marks, aggregated for best results.

AUDIT FIRM'S NAME:_____

LOCATION:_____TOTAL AWARDED:_____

No.	CRITERIA BEING ASSESSED ON	MARKS AWARDED (OUT OF 5)	SECTION SUB-TOTAL (A)	WEIGHT (B)	TOTAL (AxB)
SECTION 1 : FIRM OVERVIEW (award each line between '0' and '5' marks)					
1.1	General strength of audit firm: its local and international qualifications, affiliations, staff size, scope of services, awards, memberships etc				
1.2	Legal actions or conflicts of interest impacting firm's ability to perform required services?				
1.3	Firm's structured exposure to independent quality assurance reviews.				
1.4	Firm's "good standing" with national accounting or other regulatory body?				
1.5	Firm's international affiliation and possible access to wider operational resource(s)				
SECTION 2 : ENGAGEMENT TEAM (award each line between '0' and '5' marks)					
2.1	Reasonableness of staff mix: i.e. partners, managers, seniors, trainees (e.g. not all trainees)				
2.2	Appropriateness of roles and responsibilities of the individuals or positions listed				
2.3	Relevance and Quality of experiences & skills revealed in engagement staff CVs/Resumes				
2.4	Engagement team's working relationship fit, with our staff				
2.5	Availability of other specialists who will participate on the assignment as/if needed				

	SECTION 3 : ASSIGNMENT MANAGEMENT (award each line between '0' and '5' marks)				
3.1	How does firm's assignment management and collaboration with our staff reflect efficiency?				
3.2	Robustness and flexibility of firm's quality staff replacement, substitutions and partner rotations				
3.3	General workability of proposed timetable for the assignment and reasonable time allocations				
3.4	Practicality of firm's reporting approach as they relate to all levels of assignment				
3.5	Robustness of the firm's internal quality control and assurance procedures				

No.	CRITERIA BEING ASSESSED ON	MARKS AWARDED (OUT OF 5)	SECTION SUB-TO-TAL (A)	WEIGHT (B)	TOTAL (AxB)
	SECTION 4 : INDUSTRY EXPERIENCE (award each line between '0' and '5' marks)				
4.1	Relevance of firm's past experience (industry or jobs) to the assignement being recruited for				
4.2	Quality of firm's clientele, their similarty to our organisation and references received				
4.3	Relevance of high risk areas noted for fraud or financial misappropriation				
4.4	Reasonable accuracy of current international development sector trends identified by firm				
4.5	Firm's Clarity & relevance on specific national statutory requirements likely to impact audit?				

SECTION 5 : METHODOLOGY (award each line between '0' and '5' marks)					
5.1	Completeness of audit plan, scope, planning, audit procedures, timetable, and other matters.				
5.2	Relevance and viability of firm's advanced audit-related technologies.				
5.3	Practicality and humanness of firm's approach to resolving engagement problems that arise				
5.4	Opportunity for proposed audit approach to deliver value-added rewards				
5.5	Robustness of firm's procedures to review computerized and/or manual internal controls				
SECTION 6 : FEES AND OTHER EXPENSES (award each line between '0' and '5' marks)					
6.1	Reasonable match between fee charged and services covered				
6.2	Other out of pocket expenses to be charged on assignment and any related contingencies				
6.3	Flexibility in fee adjustments and ability to accommodate variations in services required				
6.4	Degree to which fee charges are reliably stable, barring major economic changes in the interim				
6.5	Reasonableness of basis for fee increases in subsequent years				
SECTION 7 : JUSTIFICATIONS (award each line between '0' and '5' marks)					
7.1	Attractiveness 1 to award audit job to this firm				
7.2	Attractiveness 2 to award audit job to this firm				
7.3	Attractiveness 3 to award audit job to this firm				
7.4	Attractiveness 4 to award audit job to this firm				
7.5	Attractiveness 5 to award audit job to this firm				

ASSESSED BY (FULL NAME):_____

SIGNATURE:..**DATE:** _____ / _____ / _____

2.

SAMPLE PROCUREMENT POLICY
FOR FIELD OFFICES

1.0 INTRODUCTION

This document is intended to provide a consistently applied procurement framework, enabling staff of **xxxxx** to maximize the Value-for-Money of every procurement activity. It will ensure robust financial control over its procurement and provide best value for efficient and transparent procurements every time.

Procurement is NOT just contained in the act of buying an item. In summary, it involves everything that needs doing to ensure that all procurements are for the right product/service, of the right quality and quantity, bought at the right time for the right price, from the right source and delivered to the right place. It encompasses planning, scheduling, policy interpretation, research, negotiation, selection, processing and even disposal. Above all, procurement requires the understanding of procedures to be followed during the process and the cooperation of all individuals and departments.

This document is designed to ensure that **xxxxx**:

- Conducts procurement within the scope of Generally Accepted Accounting Principles *(GAAP)*.
- Procures the appropriate goods, materials or services.
- Procures the correct quality at an advantageous price.
- Avoids any unnecessary or duplicate procurement.
- Always has sufficiently planned funds available to cover procurement.
- Conducts procurement that is allowable under donor terms and **xxxxx** rules.
- Conducts each procurement in a fully transparent and documented manner

2.0 POLICY FOUNDATIONS OF PROCUREMENT

The entire procurement process rests on the core operational foundations below. They form the integral components of this procurement policy's effective deployment and should at all times be borne inn mind:

1. Staff of **xxxxx,** need to familiarize themselves with the entirety of this procurement policy and also of donor procurement regulations applicable to related project(s). It is most important that all staff understand how to access procurement services, how the process works and what their own roles and responsibilities in the process are.

2. Throughout the procurement procedures, clear demarcations of authority and responsibility must be maintained through a well thought-out segregation of duties.

3. Given the many opportunities that procurement presents for real or perceived fraud, it is important that both staff involved directly with procurement and programme staffs, who are indirectly responsible for procurement, conduct themselves with the highest integrity and transparency.

4. All personnel involved in **xxxxx's** procurement activities will be fully conversant with their role within the procedures as well as the limits of their responsibilities and authority.

5. "Total Cost" must be considered *(not just the price tag)* in arriving at the final decision on suppliers or other procurement components. There are often hidden costs involved in making a procurement, much of which relates to staff time, e.g. the costs associated with:

   - Finding suppliers, placing orders and communications with them.
   - Risk of product failure.
   - Defining accurate need specifications.
   - Returning the product if it is not right and spending time without an item.
   - Setting up a supplier on the finance system.
   - Processing payment to suppliers.

3.0 CONFLICT OF INTEREST

All employees must be aware of what constitutes a "conflict of interest" and the procedures to follow should such a situation arise.

No employee, officer, or agent of **xxxxx** shall participate in the selection, award or administration of procurement or contracts where to his or her knowledge the employee, his or her immediate family, or partner has a financial or governance interest in the supplier's organization. Employees, officers, and agents of **xxxxx** shall neither solicit nor accept cash, gratuities, favors, or anything of monetary value from suppliers or potential suppliers. Employees or agents of **xxxxx** who knowingly violate this policy will be subject to disciplinary and / or legal actions as deemed appropriate.

If at any time during the selection, award or administration of procurement or contracts, an employee, officer or agent of **xxxxx** becomes aware of their conflict of interest with the supplier, the matter should be reported to a higher officer overseeing the procurement process for an immediate assessment to be made. The employees, officer or agent of **xxxxx** should also voluntarily withdraw temporarily from any such ongoing activity until a final confirmation has been determined regarding whether or not they do have a conflict of interest.

4.0 GENERAL CODE OF ETHICS

In order to ensure that this policy demonstrates an acceptable level of integrity, all **xxxxx** employees with or without designated purchasing or contracting authority should understand and observe the Code of Ethics below:

1. Ensure that the best interests, objectives and policies of **xxxxx** always come first.

2. Avoid the intent and *appearance* of unethical or compromising practice in relationships, actions, and communication.

3. Refrain from any private business or professional activity that would create a conflict between personal interests and the interests of **xxxxx**.

4. Refrain from soliciting or accepting money, loans, credits, or prejudicial discounts, gifts, entertainment, favors, or services from present or potential suppliers that might influence, or appear to influence procurement decisions.

5. Conduct business with potential and current suppliers in an atmosphere of good faith, devoid of intentional misrepresentation.

6. Promote fair, ethical, and legal trade practices.

7. Refrain from reciprocal agreements that restrain competition.

8. Know and obey the letter and spirit of laws governing the procurement function of **xxxxx**.

5.0 ESTABLISHING PROCUREMENT RESPONSIBILITIES

It is important that clear responsibilities are assigned for some core elements of the procurement cycle. It is equally essential that **xxxxx** staff, and other project related personnel be fully conversant with their role within the procedures as well as the limits of their responsibilities and authority:

No	PROCUREMENT SYSTEM / ACTIVITY	RESPONSIBLE PERSON OR ROLE
1	General management and oversight of the procurement function, including developing and implementing controls to effectively monitor and manage procurement practices	
2	Locating sources of supply consistent with **xxxxx** and donor policies and regulations & selecting suppliers	
3	Avoiding the procurement of duplicate or unnecessary items	
4	Meeting the budgetary, and delivery requests of requesting staff.	
5	Initiating, conducting and concluding negotiations for the procurement of goods and services.	

6	Committing **xxxxx** for the procurement of goods and services subject to **xxxxx** Policies.	
7	Recommending changes in quality, quantity, or type of material requisitioned and suggesting suitable alternatives if it is in the best interests of **xxxxx**.	
8	Developing and supporting standard specifications and processes for goods and services to provide improved service, quantity pricing and reduced time / administrative costs.	
9	Maintaining adequate documentation of procurement transactions and procurement contracts for archival and audit purposes	
10	Ensuring that procurement orders and contracts are subject to appropriate reviews and approvals, and contain all necessary information, conditions, and signatures to adequately protect **xxxxx**.	
11	Developing and implementing controls to effectively monitor and manage procurement practices	
12	Providing reports to effectively monitor and manage purchasing performance.	

6.0 DOCUMENTATION OF PROCUREMENT ACTIVITIES

Full documentation should occur throughout every cycle of procurement. This is the only means that **xxxxx** has, of managing its procurement process and demonstrating to donors and auditors that funds are being responsibly committed. A completed procurement must be supported with a fully cross-referenced documentation *(whether in e-version or hardcopy)*. Any anomalies or deviations from policy or procedure in procurement must be documented. Full supporting documentation will answer any question that an auditor or external examiner may raise.

xxxxx procurement documentation basically mirrors each step of the procurement process and if employed correctly will allow effective management and transparency of procurement activities.

As well as knowing *how* to correctly complete the various forms, Procurement staff should understand the *purpose* of the forms. This will enable them to use the forms appropriately and to make any necessary modifications for specific procurement.

7.0 COMMITMENT AND AUTHORIZATION SCHEDULE

The **xxxxx** Authorization Schedule establishes and documents the levels and type of authority accorded to designated **xxxxx** staff. It defines the levels of authorization for financial commitments that may be entered into on behalf of **xxxxx**. These levels of authority should be specific to individual projects where there is a portfolio of more than one project. This will ensure that staff only holds signing authorizations over their own budgets. New components and authorization columns can be added but this must first be approved by a responsible official within **xxxxx**.

7.1 AUTHORIZATION SCHEDULE

Example

Staff Name	Title	Authority Limit $/£/X/Y	Budgetary Responsibility	Approve Procurement Request	Authorize Cash / Bank	Sub Grant / Donor Agreement	Authorize Accounting transfer	Other
Sam Jumbosi	Country Director	30,000	Media Project Code:	Yes	Yes	Yes	Yes	

This schedule may not be circumvented in any way. Procurement or payments may not be split in order to avoid obtaining the correct level of approval. The act of splitting procurement or payment requests through intention or negligence will be viewed as a serious disciplinary offense.

By signing a document(s), managers (or the listed responsible persons) are explicitly stating that they have fully reviewed the content of such documents for accuracy and where applicable, for compliance in all applicable respects.

7.2 STANDARD CYCLE OF PROCUREMENT

The following section gives a brief description of **xxxxx** procurement process:

- A need is identified
- Specifications and estimated price are established
- Funding source(s) is determined
- A Procurement Request is raised
- The intended procurement is reviewed and approved
- The appropriate procurement mechanism is selected
- Supplier offers are solicited / received.
- A supplier is selected and a Procurement Order or contract is issued.
- Goods are received and inspected.
- Supplier is paid.
- Goods are delivered to end-destination or stock

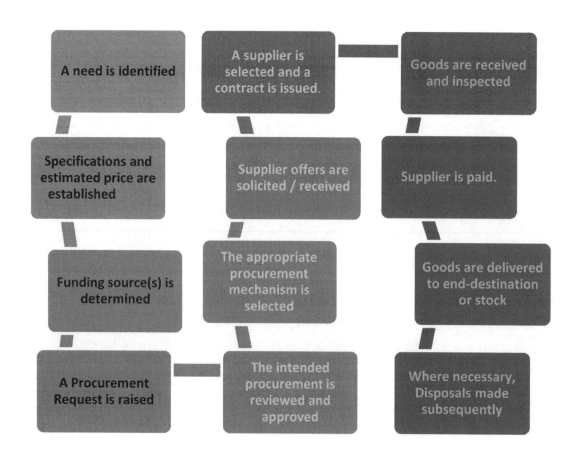

8.0 BASIC PROCUREMENT PROCESSES AND DOCUMENTS

8.1 PROCUREMENT / PROCUREMENT REQUESTS (PR)

PRs may be generated by any **xxxxx** staff member, with due regard for the appropriate division of responsibilities outlined above. The PR is the internal mechanism that initiates a procurement cycle. It must document:

- The specifications and nature of required materials or services.
- The financial codes covering the procurement.
- The maximum commitment for the procurement.
- The review and approval process.
- Authorization to initiate the purchasing process.

The PR is generic, and serves for services as well as supplies and equipment. A PR document will be produced for all procurement.

Where actual costs exceed the approved Procurement Request (PR) amount, Logistics are authorized to proceed with the procurement provided that the difference is the littlest of 10% of the original value estimated. Cost differences greater than this must be re-authorized by means of the approving manager counter-signing the amended original PR.

XXXXX ORGANIZATION NAME
PROCUREMENT/ PROCUREMENT REQUEST (PR)

P. O. Box 3345
Kwazimba City Post
Kwazu Mekol District
People's Republic of Gima

Date:..

Project/Office Name Procurement is requested for:	**Project/Office Code** (Budget/Accounting):

The specifications and nature of required items or services (including technical details)	

Justification for Procurement:	**The maximum committed amount:**
	Procurement method suggested:

Notes from Financial Review and Authorisation:	

Requesting Staff	Finance Review Officer	Procurement Authorizer
Signature	Signature	Signature
	My review confirms: ***PR has been completed correctly and that the mathematics used are correct ***The costs for the intended procurement have been allocated to the correct budget(s) ***Funds are available to cover the cost of the intended procurement	**My authorization confirms:** ***the information in and documentation for this request is complete ***Procurement is necessary to meet program or operational goals. ***Technically appropriate for the intended use. ***Allowable under grant terms or HQ requirements

8.2 REQUEST FOR QUOTATION (RFQ)

A Request for Quotation (RFQ) is used to solicit offers from vendors *(potential suppliers)* for items or services to be procured. It will detail the nature and procurement conditions of the materials or services sought.

All suppliers must receive the same RFQ information in order that they all have the same ability to respond. Failure to do so can give the impression certain suppliers are being disadvantaged by not having sufficient information to respond competitively. An RFQ will be produced for all procurement that require written quotations / bids

Note that the RFQ is used to solicit information on goods and services that are clearly defined. There will be instances when the job or service details are not fully known and the suppliers are required to offer solutions or options. In these cases the Request for Proposal (RFP) is used. This is still basically an RFQ but is a better format for the purpose. The RFP is also the mechanism used as part of selecting contracted suppliers.

8.3 REQUEST FOR PROPOSAL (RFP)

The RFP format can vary widely depending on what is being requested. At its simplest it will look very much like the standard RFQ. Instead of stating the item(s) required, it would describe the required result or performance and ask the supplier to suggest a solution.

In cases where it is necessary or advantageous to seek offers from as many suppliers as possible, the RFQ/P process takes on a slightly different format. Rather than giving RFQ/Ps directly to a limited number of suppliers, a public announcement of some sort (newspaper, trade journal, radio, websites etc.) is used to reach as many suppliers as possible. Basically suppliers are informed briefly of what goods or services **xxxxx** wants, and are asked to let **xxxxx** know if they are interested in submitting an offer. This is known as an Open Bib/Tender process.

The request to the suppliers is called an **Invitation to Bid, or Invitation to Tender (or Call for Expressions of Interest).** Whatever it is called, the function is the same – to invite a wide number of suppliers to quote for the required goods or services in order to maximize competition.

Once a supplier has indicated that they wish to participate in the process, they will receive an RFP, detailing the goods or services required and the procedure for making an offer.

It may not always be necessary to invite suppliers through an open process in which case the same documents can be submitted directly to known suppliers.

8.4 BID ANALYSIS SUMMARY (BA)

The Bid Analysis (BA) is the document used to summarize and compare supplier offers. It also documents and details justification for the selection of a given supplier. It is important that supplier justification is objective and verifiable as this is an important part of competitive procurement and therefore subject to audit scrutiny. Certain procurement will require a "double" justification. For example, purchasing a vehicle will entail justifying the choice of manufacturer/model and then the choice of supplier.

8.5 CONTRACTS

A contract documents the nature, terms and conditions of a transaction as agreed to by both (or all) parties. A contract represents a legal commitment between xxxxx and the supplier. In simple terms a full contract will be drawn up when payments, delivery or guarantees are to be made/provided wholly or in installments at some point in the future. There should be a contract:

- if at any point in a transaction either or both of the parties are vulnerable to loss, should the agreement not be met.
- when no other simple document suffices as a full documentation of the agreement.
- when non-standard **xxxxx** terms and conditions are agreed to.
- when the procurement value is equal to or greater than an internally set amount or threshold.
- when a "service" is to be procured.

The contract will be as detailed as possible and serve as the Terms of Reference.

8.6 SUPPLIER INVOICES

An invoice is the suppliers' document against which payment is made, by **xxxxx**. The invoice must detail the nature of goods / services supplied, terms and method of payment and the amount demanded, as well as details of the vendor's name, address and contact details. The invoice must match the corresponding procurement request or order placed. **xxxxx** should only make payments to a vendor on receipt of a verifiable invoice.

8.7 TYPES OF PROCUREMENT MECHANISM

Depending on the type and value of the intended procurement and the time frame available, there are a number of methods of undertaking procurement. The basic premise is that the more suppliers that participate, the more competition is generated so the better the offers received. Following are the common mechanisms in descending order of competitiveness.

Open Bids: Invitation to all and potentially interested suppliers; invitation is published in appropriate national or international publications or trade journals. All offers are included in the selection. Used for large-volume procurement exceeding **Y-amount** or a set donor threshold. Will generally yield better pricing than limited bidding but requires a lot of time and preparation.

Restricted Bid: Invitation to all interested suppliers, but only those deemed qualified are invited to tender. Low bid or VFM offer accepted. This is one of the most commonly used for large-volume procurement. Generally yields reasonable price offers, and involves a moderate amount of work.

Negotiated: (**Also called Competitive Quotes**) A small number (typically 3 or 4) of potential suppliers are approached and specific price or service arrangements are directly negotiated. This method is most applicable to low-volume procurement. Delivery times are short and the volume of work that goes into this is minimal. Useful if **xxxxx** already has a list of relevant suppliers.

Direct: This is the simplest procurement method. Items are procured from a single supplier at the quoted price. This should really only be applicable to low value or emergency procurement. Pricing may not be the best on the market but delivery time is short. Workload involved is low.

Sealed Bid: This is more a requirement than a procurement mechanism. It is used to preserve the integrity of supplier offers and thereby fairness of the selection.

In all methods, documentation and conduct of procurement, staff must be transparent. Any perception of unfair or corrupt practices may well discourage reputable suppliers with the effect that **xxxxx** may not receive the best products or prices.

9.0 SUPPLIER CATEGORIES

9.1 AD HOC SUPPLIERS

Suppliers used on an infrequent basis mainly for direct small value procurement or who are selected on an individual procurement basis, usually as a result of a competitive quote process. The value of the procurement and / or donor procurement regulations will determine the appropriate process to use.

9.2 AUTHORIZED SUPPLIERS

These are suppliers who have been *pre-qualified* by **xxxxx** to provide price quotations. These suppliers will be established for goods and services used on a fairly regular basis. Working with a limited number of reliable and reputable suppliers allows closer monitoring of pricing and relationships. It cuts procurement time. Some donor regulations actually require the establishment of Authorized Vendors.

Identifying suppliers for an Authorized list involves the use of open well thought-out surveys and in most cases, interviews and third party recommendations combined. Usually, a selection panel will review the offers and determine which suppliers meet the criteria for pre-qualified status. Subsequently, new suppliers, or suppliers wishing to be reconsidered will be reviewed on an individual basis. It is also possible to use the results of an RFP process for a specific procurement to pre-qualify vendors.

The database / file for authorized suppliers will include the following information:

- company name and address
- name of the manager / contact person
- phone / fax / email coordinates
- type of goods or services offered
- basis of pricing (list, catalog, prevailing market etc.)
- company capacity (staffing, stock levels, etc.)
- date of first entry into the register
- date of last information update
- **xxxxx** comment on the basis of the collected data

9.3 CONTRACTED SUPPLIERS

Contracted Suppliers are suppliers with whom **xxxxx** has a formal contractual relationship. These suppliers are selected after a formal RFP (Request for Proposal) process and are used for materials or services procured on a regular basis. Contracts are established for defined categories of goods under an agreed price structure for a specified period. Contracts may only be established for items or equipment that **xxxxx** *commonly* procures for its activities. i.e. it may not be established for occasional or ad-hoc procurement. This will typically be for administrative or vehicle supplies and services, or project supplies.

For any of the above categories, the supplier must, at a minimum

- Be a legally registered company or professional in good standing
- Be eligible to conduct business by any specific donor standard
- Be of sound reputation (verify with other agencies).
- Be financially sound or show low financial risk to being going concern
- Possess stocks, production, or service delivery capacity to support **xxxxx**'s needs

xxxxx staff that are found to be intentionally, knowingly, or negligently trading with vendors who do not meet these criteria will be subject to disciplinary action.

10.0 REGULAR SUPPLIERS' APPRAISAL & RECORDS

10.1 TERM APPRAISALS

In order to achieve consistent value for money in the use of suppliers, it is essential that suppliers are routinely monitored. **xxxxxx**'s engagement with all suppliers whether contractual or mutual, has to be regularly reviewed at least every three years. This must be agreed in the contract *(where they are contracted)* with the supplier from the outset. To do so, the following should be considered:

- Is the supplier providing good quality products and or service?
- Have they been reasonably delivering on time?
- How do they deal with problems or concerns raised by **xxxxxx**?
- Are there insurance implications for this supplier?
- Have there been more than a few issues of sub-standard products/services?
- Is the supplier's internal administration efficient when dealing with **xxxxxx**?
- Are there terms in the original contracts that have become irrelevant?

10.2 SUPPLIER INFORMATION FILES

A good Supplier Information file will contain:

Full legal name of the supplier,
>   Business registration no.
>   Mailing address
>   Location address
>   Telephone, website, Skype & email

Historical Data,
>   Ownership of the business and date founded.
>   Number of manufacturing facilities
>   Number of employees
>   Names of parent, subsidiary or affiliated companies

Management Data,
>   Names of senior executives
>   Corporate memberships in Trade Associations
>   Industrial certifications

Supply Information,
>   Management and quality assurance techniques
>   Information on goods and services supplied.
>   Delivery times
>   Warranties and after service facilities
>   Packing and shipping capabilities
>   Payment terms

Corporate Brochures,
>   Product information and data sheets, other available literature

References,
>   Current and recent major clients
>   Goods or services supplied.
>   Value of orders

Comments on Past Performance,
>   Documented information on past orders with **xxxxxx**

10.3 PAYING A SUPPLIER

A complete set of original procurement documentation will be required to support payments to suppliers. This documentation may be inspected by internal and external auditors and also forms part of the *"checks and balances"* of the procurement process:

- That the procurement was authorized.
- That the correct procurement method was employed (RFQ or RFP etc., BA and support docs),
- That the goods or services ordered, were actually received and,
- That quantity and quality of the goods or services corresponded to those ordered.

All documentation will be fully and accurately completed, cross-referenced and verifiable.

11.0 PROCUREMENT MATRIX

As an excellent tool for ensuring that procurement standards are easily assessable to members or associates of **xxxxxx**, we recommend that the following table is fully completed to suit particular contexts and other local regulations. More rows and parameters can be added depending on need

Value of procurement	=<$ABC	>$ABC & =<$EFG	>$EFG & =<$HIJ	>$ HIJ & =<$KLM	>$KLM
Is a detailed Need assessment needed at this level of procurement?					
Level at which xxxxxx is most exposed to financial misconduct					
Authorisation Needed at this level?					
Which post should authorise at this level?					

Degree of formality that applies at this level	Low	Low - Medium	Medium	Medium – High	High
Basis of Supplier Payment	Receipt or other similar	Receipt / invoice	Invoice	Invoice	Invoice
File Held for Supplier?	Not	Not essential	Good Practice	Essential	Essential
Is Conflict of Interest a Central Consideration?	Only as a general principle		Advised	Yes	Yes
Does this level require a regular Appraisal of Suppliers?	Only as a general principle		Advised	Yes	Yes
Steps to making a procurement					
Level of detail required to support specifying the product or service	Use supplier catalogues, price lists, **xxxxxx** internal specs.	Special requirements identified.	Full Spec involving all likely users	Full Spec involving all likely users	Full Spec involving all likely users
Identify potential suppliers	Current suppliers with good history	Extend to new suppliers for higher value items.	Always consider new suppliers.	Always consider new suppliers.	Always consider new suppliers.
What method of Procurement should be adopted					
Recommended mode of Procurement	Direct	Negotiated/ Competitive quotes	Restricted	Open or closed Bids/ tender	Open or closed Bids/ tender
Competitive Quotes?:	Not applicable	Recommended	Compulsory unless Tendering	Some level or form of Competitive Bid	Compulsory use of Bids
Requiring a Bid or Tender?	Not applicable	Not applicable	Recommended	Recommended	Compulsory
Researching for a Supplier		Desk research/Calls/Other departments / industry recommendations		Desk research; obtain references (internal or external) including financial	

12.0 GUIDELINE TO MAKING A PROCUREMENT DECISION

Before procurement *(no matter the size or volume)* it is recommended that the following list is considered before a concrete decision to proceed is made:

Do I really need to procure this good/service? (Is the "need" right?)
- Does **xxxxx** already have the resource elsewhere that one could make use of?
- Can the service be provided using voluntary help or the goods obtained by donation?

What do I need? (Is the potential "product or service" right for the intended purpose?)
- What do I need this product or service to do and does it meet those needs?
- Can I find better value for money for **xxxxx** by getting something else?
- How long will this item be of value to **xxxxx** for?
- Are there any contracts, service agreements or restrictions associated?

Will anyone else need something similar? (Is the quality right?)
- Have I over/under specified the quality, or is it "fit for purpose".
- Who else will be using this or a similar product?
- Who should be invited to agree or have an input in the specification?

How much do I need? (Is the quantity right?)
- Am I considering the quantity that would be enough for the duration it is required for?
- If I procure more than I need, will storage costs make the overall procurement too expensive?
- Would anyone else need it and can the quantities be optimized by combining our needs?

Where do I need it? (Is the place I need it for, right?)
- Where will this product or service be used and is it the best place?
- Where will it be stored and what safety considerations are needed?
- How and how far will it be transported?

When do I need it? (Is time/period I need it for right?)

- When will this product be out of date or obsolete?
- When do I need it to be working and will the lead time allow it to arrive in time?
- When will I no longer need this product or service?

Who from? (Is the source I intend to use, right?)

- Is there a centralized purchasing arrangement?
- Is there a preferred supplier or one that has been used in other sections of **xxxxx**?
- Can colleagues who have made similar procurement provide advice?
- Does the supplier have the right credentials to supply this particular requirement?
- Does the supplier offer post procurement support if it becomes needed?

How much do I pay? (Is the pricing for this supply, right?)

- What form of procurement is being used and is it in line with value and internal requirements?
- Are there ways I can take advantage of discounts?
- What are the payment terms and how best can they be negotiated to the advantage of **xxxxx**?

3.

PARTNER FINANCIAL SELF-ASSESSMENT
QUESTIONNAIRE

INTRODUCTION

The Financial Self-Assessment Questionnaire helps gauge how healthy a partner's (or potential partner's) financial management system and environment, is. The term "Self-Assessment" implies the questionnaire can either be used by yourself or by the potential partner, as a first level assessment, without the need for a financial expert. Generally, based on its results, a decision can then be made whether a detailed due diligence is required to be carried out by a financial expert. That decision to go a step beyond the results of this questionnaire will also depend on the environment being worked in (*e.g. some countries have cash-economies or lack basic banking services – increasing the risks around cash handling*); and also, the size of funds being committed to the potential partner (*e.g. for a $3,000 commitment to the partner, all the components of the questionnaire may not be required*)

Money is the lifeblood of any organisation. Little can be achieved without it, it is a scarce resource and must be used well. That means working with good financial management.

A WORD OF CAUTION

This questionnaire only provides a general indication of the health of partner's financial management. It is not an exhaustive list of all aspects of financial management. It is not an audit and it does not describe a standard set of procedures which will always be completely relevant in every situation. Every partner is different and financial management systems must reflect this. A 'one size fits all' approach will never work – what is important for one organisation may not be appropriate for another.

But the key aspects of good practice should be the same for most partner organisations most of the time. The questionnaire focuses on those key aspects. They are the foundation stones of good practice.

USING THE QUESTIONNAIRE

The questionnaire is a series of just over forty simple questions. Discuss each statement with the relevant member(s) of staff or verify with a document and record whether it is "always true", "mostly true", "sometimes true" or "never true" in the organisation being reviewed.

The responses are explained and given a score as follows:

Response	Explanation	Score
Always true	True 100% of the time	5
Mostly true	True between 71% and 99% of the time	4
Sometimes true	True between 20% and 70% of the time	1
Never true	True less than 20% of the time	0

Circle your score for each statement on the questionnaire. Then add up your scores for each section. That's it! By comparing your scores to the table on the *'interpreting your score'* section, you can tell how healthy the partner's financial management is.

Name of Partner:	
Name of Reviewer:	
Date of Review:	
Nature of Partnership:	

SECTION 1: BASIC SYSTEMS

A) Supporting Documents
Every financial transaction should be backed up by a 'supporting document', e.g. a bill, invoice or receipt. This is the evidence that a specific transaction has taken place.

No.	Area of Review	Always	Mostly	Some-times	Never
1.1	A supporting document is available for every expenditure transaction for the current financial year. [test 10 random ones]	5	4	1	0
1.2	Supporting document is available for every income transaction for any selected year/month. [test 5 random]	5	4	1	0
1.3	Supporting documents are filed, so that it is easy to find any document when it is needed. [see it for yourself]	5	4	1	0
1.4	All bank statements for each bank account are regularly filed and regular reconciliations are done. [see it for yourself]	5	4	1	0
1.5	Supporting documents and bank statements are kept for at least the previous 2 years. [see old files for yourself]	5	4	1	0

B) Cashbooks & Financial Records

Every transaction should be recorded in a cashbook or some financial journal (*whether manual or electronic*). A cashbook or journal is just a list of the monies that an organisation has spent / received. It can be kept on paper or on a computer.

No.	Area of Review	Always	Mostly	Some-times	Never
1.6	The date, description and amount of every transaction are recorded in a cashbook. [see it for yourself]	5	4	1	0
1.7	All financial books are updated at least once per month. [see it for yourself]	5	4	1	0
1.8	A separate book (or column in the same book) is kept for each bank & petty cash account. [see it for yourself]	5	4	1	0

C) Accounts Codes

Accounting works by assigning codes to the transactions entered in the financial books. The codes allow transactions to be easily classified together and reports, produced e.g. so that all transactions relating to a particular type of expenditure and/or grant or donor can be traced separately. It also allows transactions to be classified by say, the donor funds it is supported by, the specific project it was spent on etc. These set of accounting codes that an organisation uses is called its *"Chart of Accounts".*

No.	Area of Review	Always	Mostly	Some-times	Never
1.9	A basic Chart of Accounts is used to code all the financial transactions in the organisation's records.	5	4	1	0
1.10	The Chart of Accounts is linked to budgets and traceable to the preparation of financial reports.	5	4	1	0
1.11	Transactions can be classified by project, or activity or income source?	5	4	1	0

Total score for BASIC SYSTEMS	

SECTION 2: INTERNAL CONTROLS

Organisations use different internal controls (i.e. a system of checks and balances) to ensure project funds are used properly and that they can achieve their objectives. This list sets out a selection of controls. It is not an exhaustive list – but it includes controls for key areas of financial management.

Note: the other sections of the questionnaire are also important controls in themselves. E.g., supporting documents prove that a transaction has happened.

No.	Area of Review	Always	Mostly	Some-times	Never
2.1	All cash kept in the office is kept under lock [inspect it]	5	4	1	0
2.2	All bank accounts are held in the name of the partner, not in the name of individuals. [see statements yourself]	5	4	1	0
2.3	There is a written or known policy setting out which members of staff can authorise expenditure. [if not written, ask more than 2 persons to be sure]	5	4	1	0
2.4	Each transaction is authorised by the appropriate member(s) of staff. [sample, match and assure yourself]	5	4	1	0
2.5	Staff, check that goods and services bought by the partner have been received before bills are paid.	5	4	1	0
2.6	Cheques are not signed before details are written on it and supporting documents checked (i.e. no signed blank cheques) [inspect cheque books for yourself if available]	5	4	1	0
2.7	Staff salaries (including advances/loans) are checked by a senior officer every time before they are executed.	5	4	1	0
2.8	Financial duties are split between different members of staff. i.e. no 1 person is responsible for most financial recordings, banking, authorisations, payments etc	5	4	1	0
2.9	The balance in the cashbook is reconciled to the balance on the bank statement every month for every bank account and differences identified/explained.	5	4	1	0
2.10	The balance in the cashbook or other financial books is reconciled to the physical amount of cash in the office every month for every cash account.	5	4	1	0
2.11	All reconciliations are checked by a senior officer	5	4	1	0
2.12	All assets owned by the organisation are recorded in an Asset Register.	5	4	1	0
2.13	An audit or some other Financial Review is carried out at least once a year by a qualified external auditor or equally qualified person.	5	4	1	0

Total score for INTERNAL CONTROLS

SECTION 3: PLANNING

A) Budgets

Budgets have a crucial role to play in strong financial management. For budgets to be useful, they must be accurate and complete. That means that they have to be based on a realistic assessment of the activities that you expect to carry out and of how you expect to pay for them.

No.	Area of Review	Always	Mostly	Some-times	Never
3.1	Budgets are prepared for the costs of running the organisation every year.	5	4	1	0
3.2	Budgets are prepared in consultation with beneficiaries and donors for all projects prior to commencement	5	4	1	0
3.4	Budgets include enough income to cover all planned expenditure; shortfalls noted and funded alternatively	5	4	1	0

B) Cashflow forecast

A cashflow forecast is as important as a budget. The cash-flow forecast tells you when receipts and payments will happen, what periods cash shortfalls and excesses will occur in.

No.	Area of Review	Always	Mostly	Some-times	Never
3.6	Cash-flow forecast is prepared, for the next six months period/other timeframe	5	4	1	0

C) Donors

Donors like to fund specific projects with specific budgets. But often, partners work with several different donors at the same time. It is very important to keep track of which donor is funding which project (or part of a project). It is very bad practice to 'use' money received from one donor for another donor's project. In fact, this is often illegal **("contra funding")**. Accepting money from two different donors for precisely the same costs is also illegal **("double dipping).**

No.	Area of Review	Always	Mostly	Some-times	Never
3.7	Is funding from each donor and the expenditures related to them separately identifiable? Check to see funding from different donors is held in separate Bank Accounts. Where they are all held in the same account, check to see that the organisation has a clear mechanism to identify each donor's funds and also its related expenditures. **(also crosscheck donor incomes received to donor contracts and payment notification letters/emails).**	5	4	1	0
3.8	There are enough funds to cover all the expenditure necessary to run the organisation and projects.	5	4	1	0
3.9	Different donors are not funding the same costs on the same project. Sample some similar expenditure types e.g. a specific staff cost and see if it can be traced to expenditure recorded under more than one donor. Except e.g. if the employee is spending a part of their working time on more than one project.	5	4	1	0
3.10	The organisation can continue to operate even if any single donor stops providing funding **(check that the organization is not dependent on only one donor. Otherwise, question its sustainability).**	5	4	1	0

Total score for **PLANNING**	

SECTION 4: REPORTING

Managers, beneficiaries, trustees and donors rely on financial reports to understand an organisation or a project's financial position:

- Managers need accurate internal reports to know where money has been spent and whether they are on track financially, or that there is enough funds to pay the salaries and bills in the coming months.
- Beneficiaries need financial reports to know whether money is being spent on their real needs.

- Donors need reports to monitor the use of their funds.
- Government uses reports to establish that Statutory requirements are being followed and that an organisation or project is operating in line with it's development agenda.

As a minimum, the monthly/quarterly/half-yearly/yearly financial reports (for each donor) should include details of all income received and expenditure made during the period and any balances held in cash and/or bank. Other important components can include: a variance report, explaining the reasons for differences between budgeted and actual expenditures and a cashflow forecast.

No.	Area of Review	Always	Mostly	Some-times	Never
4.1	Senior manager(s) regularly review the financial position of the organisation and of projects by matching their budgets with actual up-to-date data, reacting to differences positive or negative	5	4	1	0
4.2	Financial reports are submitted to donors in the right format and on time. (compare the reporting timeframe in the contract to actual report submission dates of past reports).	5	4	1	0
4.3	Financial reports are submitted to the right government agency in the right format and on time.	5	4	1	0
4.4	Internal records and management reports agree with donor reports and reports sent to government. (compare the samples of details in old reports, with corresponding records of the organisation/project).	5	4	1	0

Total score for REPORTING	

SECTION 5: STAFF

Good financial management relies on good staff. Staff, need to have the right skills and support to carry out their responsibilities. This means that managers need to know about financial management as well as finance staff.

No.	Area of Review	Always	Mostly	Some-times	Never
5.1	The board / trustees include someone who has the skills needed to oversee financial matters that arise.	5	4	1	0
5.2	The finance staff have the skills *(and qualifications)* needed to carry out all financial activities.	5	4	1	0
5.3	There are enough finance staff to carry out all of the financial activities and keep a balance on segregation of duties	5	4	1	0
5.4	Managers and other staff have a basic understanding of budgets and to implement internal controls.	5	4	1	0
5.5	All staff receive training and ongoing support they need to carry out their financial responsibilities.	5	4	1	0

Total score for STAFF	

NOTES & HIGHLIGHTS

_____

_____

_____

_____

_____

_____

_____

_____

_____

_____

_____

TOTAL FINAL SCORE	

INTERPRETING YOUR SCORE

Record your score for each section in this table. Then compare it to the columns on the right to gauge how much risk you are facing.

Section	Score [enter scores]	High Risk	Medium Risk	Low Risk
1. Basic systems		0 - 18	19 - 40	41 - 55
2. Internal control		0 - 21	22 - 52	53 - 65
3. Planning		0 - 13	14 - 33	34 - 40
4. Reporting		0 - 6	7 - 16	17 - 20
5. Staff		0 - 9	10 - 20	21 - 25
Total Score		**0 - 67**	**68 - 161**	**162 - 205**

Total score is over 161

If the total score is over 161 then well done to the partner! It's basic financial management is in good shape. The risks of not being able to complete your work because of financial problems are low. *But, one cannot afford to relax.*

Total score is between 68 and 161 *(inclusive)*

If your total score is between 68 and 161 (inclusive) then partner's financial management is not too bad but not too good either. There is a medium level of risk that financial problems will prevent you from carrying out your work. This is a cause for concern. *Low scoring areas require immediate attention from managers.*

Total score is less than 68

If your total score is lower than 68 then partner has problems. It's financial management is not in good health. There is a high risk that partner will face financial problems in the near future. *Issues need to be resolved before proceeding with partnership further*

CONCLUDING REMARKS

1. Depending on your risk tolerance level and depending on whether the partner has made a good overall score but shows weakness in a particular section; you could proceed with your partnership in the following manners:

   - Request improvement in their entirety **before** partnership / collaboration commences.
   - Commence the partnership / collaboration with a **clause** for improvements to be carried out by a certain date within the duration of the contract
   - Commence the partnership / collaboration with with a **clause** for regular monitoring partly or throughout the entire project

2. Where, you have requested the partner to carry out a self-assessment and submit the results to you, do bear in mind that you have an additional responsibility to ascertain by other means whether or not, the responses provided by the partner in this questionnaire are whole, truthful or fair.

4.

FUNDING AGREEMENT BETWEEN
DONOR AND GRANTEE

1. THE AGREEMENT IDENTIFICATION

In order that this Agreement is the same referred to by all parties, it is herein stated the particular credentials, by which this Agreement shall be identified to all parties:

The Fund from which this Grant is given is: _____

Donor's Reference ID(s) for this grant is: _____

The Title of Project Being Funded is: _____

_____

Beneficiary Country (ies) of Project: _____

2. THE PARTIES

This Funding Agreement, *(hereinafter referred to as "Agreement")* is between DONOR *(hereinafter referred to as "DONOR"),* [enter *name and address of* DONOR here] and or its country representation XYZ at [*address of DONOR local office*] and [*name and address of Grantee*] *(hereinafter referred to as "Grantee").*

3. CONTEXT

[*State here, the circumstances within which it became necessary for this project to be initiated*]

4. VALIDITY PERIOD OF CONTRACT

This Agreement and hence the project (or activities) it relates to enters into force on [*Enter contract start date*] and expires on [*Enter contract end date*]

5. PROJECT DESCRIPTION

The purpose of this grant is to:

[*Enter here, the summary purpose / objectives for which this grant is being awarded to the Grantee – what is it expected to achieve*]

A Project Description [*or work-plan or original proposal*] is attached as annex 1, and is incorporated into this Agreement. The grant purpose and Project Description are collectively referred to here as the "Project". They are considered to form an integral part of this Agreement. If this Agreement and the annexes contradict each other, the text of this Agreement should be used as the authoritative version.

6. GRANT FUNDING & GENERAL PROVISIONS

6.1 DONOR agrees to provide, according to the payment schedule or budgets and other terms herein, up to a total not exceeding [*state TOTAL value of grant and donor currency*] to the Grantee. The grant will amount to the local or other receiving currency amount achieved by converting this at the one or various time(s) of disbursement(s).

6.2 **The general grant provisions this Agreement is subject to are as follows:**

i.   That the Grantee is and will remain so, at all times throughout this Agreement, a fully compliant, registered charity or not for profit organisation according to the laws of the country(ies) of operation. This includes, it satisfying relevant statutory and umbrella requirements.

ii. That funds provided to the Grantee will not be spent on import or customs duties or similar, of the Government(s) whose country (ies) benefit from from the application of funds covered in this agreement, except where this has been specifically agreed to, by the DONOR;

iii. That continuation of this Agreement in each financial year will be dependent upon satisfactory progress being achieved by the Grantee and its related parties;

iv. That the Grantee covenants to take all steps appropriate to ensure no funds under this Agreement are used to provide assistance to, or otherwise support, individuals, groups or corporate persons involved in any and all forms of terrorism and sexual discrimination directly or indirectly.

v. That the Grantee agrees to ensure, that where it deals with children, adults and vulnerable people in general, it has the appropriate and effective policies and procedures in place to assure their safety, protection and rights.

7. PROJECT BUDGET

7.1   Budget Schedule

The agreed detailed budget for this contract is attached as annex 2. Listed here only, are the main summaries of the same budget:

	Main Budget Titles	Budget Allocation
1	Fixed Assets	£ 90,000
2	Personnel Costs	£ 250,000
3	Monitoring & Evaluation	£ 160,000
etc.	etc.	etc.
Total		

	Financial Year	Amount Approved
1	2014	£ 125,000
2	2015	£ 231,000
3	2016	£ 144,000
etc.	etc	etc
Total		

7.2   Budget Administration

7.2.1   The Grantee shall ensure that all expenditures made under this Agreement are actually, properly and necessarily expended in accordance with the most recently approved Budget for the project and all other provisions outlined in any other written correspondences or documentations issued by the DONOR, including this Agreement.

7.2.2   Budget line virements/changes can be made without any prior approval by the DONOR as long as the amounts being reallocated between different budget lines do not result in:

   (a) Any of the "Main Budget Heading" totals exceeding X% of their original amount or £xxx *(whichever is lower; negative or positive);*

   (b) Any individual budget line being increased/reduced by 50% or more of its original value;

   (c) The total Budget allocated for that particular year, changing.

7.2.3   Any virement/changes outside these parameters will need the DONOR's approval prior to spending.

The Grantee further agrees, such unapproved budget variations will not exceed #XX [number] individual budget line changes within any 1 year [Delete or amend this clause as appropriate]. Beyond that limit, approval must be sought from the DONOR.

7.2.4   As a result of one or more of the following conditions:

- Inability of DONOR to guarantee that funds allocated, but left unspent at the end of any project year-end will be made available for spending in the subsequent year
- Changes in project operations and focus due to lessons from monitoring/ evaluation;
- Changes in project operations and focus due to changes in the project's political, economic, social, technical and natural environments;
- Changes in project operations and focus due to uncontrollable circumstances;

It is recommended *(not conditional)* that the Grantee reviews its project activities and expenditure patterns midway through the project year and where it considers it prudent, to request a Budget Variation altogether [Delete or amend this clause as appropriate].

A Budget Variation: this involves requesting approval from the DONOR for changes to different budget lines in any given year ONLY. Effectively, the contractual budget allocation for the current year remains the same, despite the change.

A Budget Revision: this involves requesting approval from the DONOR for changes to different budget lines in the current and subsequent project years. Effectively, the contractual budget allocation for the current and/or subsequent project years will change, as a result.

7.2.5   A Budget Revision *(as outlined above)* is compulsorily required for each project at the end of every year and must culminate in the submission of a Budget Revision Request no later than XX days before the end of the project year in question. This process is an opportunity for the Grantee, after careful analysis and in-depth projections, to determine whether or not funds allocated to, but likely to remain unspent in the current project year, can JUSTIFIABLY be requested to be carried forward into following years. The Grantee doesn't need to submit any Budget Revision Request if it foresees no need to carry over current year's allocated funds [Delete or amend this clause as appropriate]

7.2.6   A <u>Budget Revision Request</u> or a <u>Budget Variation</u> will only be considered and approved if either contains (i) A Revised Budget submission and (ii) A Justification submission.

7.2.6.1 *A Revised Budget Submission*

Irrespective of the number of years the budget changes will affect (*i.e. current year for a Budget Variation or 1+ years for a Budget Revision*), it is strictly required that the revised budget being submitted MUST:

1. Be in Excel Format and in DONOR currency

2. Incorporate the same level of detail as the most recently agreed Budget

3. Cover the entire life of the project, not just the year (s) revisions will affect

4. In particular, the year(s) to be affected by the changes MUST show columns side by side for:

    - "Original Budget" (the most current, approved budget for that year);
    - The "Revised Budget" (How the Grantee wishes the new budget to look);
    - The variance between the two in donor currency; and

5. For year(s) already elapsed, Actual Expenditures must be shown against budget lines

BUDGET HEAD-INGS	Actual Ex-pend **Yr1** 2013	Orig-inal Budget **Yr2** 2014	Re-vised Budget **Yr2** 2014	Variance (Amount) **Yr2** 2014	Original Budget **Yr3** 2015	Orig-inal Budget **Yr4** 2016	TOTAL Original Budget **(All Years)**	TOTAL Revised Budget **(All Years)**	NOTES
FIXED ASSETS									
1 Nissan 4x4									1
4 Office Desk sets									
3 Dell Laptops									2

7.2.6.2 *A Justification Submission*

This submission can be made separately or in one of tabs of the Excel Budget submission referred to above. Its main purpose is to provide the necessary justifications for the changes as follows:

#	Type of Justification	Required for a Budget Variation	Required for a Budget Revision
1	For budget lines where funds are being taken from – Are these actual or anticipated underspends and if anticipated what is the justification that such underspends would have occurred in the natural progression of the project. If actual, why have they occurred?	Yes	Yes
2	For budget lines where allocations are being increased, what is the justification for increasing such budget lines? The "WHY"	Yes	Yes
3	Following on from (2) above, what added "Value" to the project, is being achieved as a result of the increased allocation	Yes	Yes
4	Where funding is being moved from a budget line (A) in the current year to another budget line (B) in subsequent year(s), what implications are there, for increased capacity requirements, whether human or otherwise, to carry out the additional work likely to result from increased budget on line B?	No	Yes

5	Where funds are being moved as in (4) above, and/or where new budget lines are being created as part of the budget changes – to what extent should these changes be reflected in the project years following? Should they be expected to recur in all following years?	No	Yes
6	Where funds are being moved from one project year to others, what mitigating actions have been put in place to ensure such reallocations do not become merely repetitive.	No	Yes

7.3   Other Budget Issues

7.3.1   DONOR will not be liable for any expenses incurred by the recipient in excess of the amounts shown in the budget (*if it has not been approved prior by* DONOR)

7.3.2   DONOR will not pay or reimburse any expenses incurred, relating to activities not included in the detailed budget or Project description, unless these have been authorised in advance by DONOR, in writing.

7.3.3   The Grantee is not authorised to contract or sub-grant to other organisations to undertake work or activities defined in the program description without prior written approval from DONOR.

7.3.4   By signing this agreement the Grantee attests that the activities and expenses covered by this agreement will not be funded by any other source than the DONOR's and that the funds allocated and disbursed for these budgeted expenses shall not be used to fund expenses related to other donor budgets, even if temporarily.

8. EXCHANGE RATES AND VARIATIONS

8.1   The DONOR requires that the Grantee has its own policies on Exchange Rates and that they are in line with Generally Accepted Accounting Principles (GAAPs).

8.2   The DONOR and Grantee by this Agreement accept, that although project budgets may have been drawn up, based on estimated exchange rates (*where applicable*), actual expenditures recorded and reported against each budget line should reflect actual exchange rates either:

        (i) at the point where funds are received into local currency;

        (ii) calculated as an average over a day, week, month, or quarter.

8.3   Where the DONOR's currency performs strongly against the Grantee currency, and as a result more local currency becomes available, the following two options should be applied:

        a. where activities relating to a particular budget line have been fully completed and yet, local funds remain unspent on such a budget line – return the unspent funds back to DONOR immediately or at the end of the year;

        b. where original activities relating to a particular budget line have been completed and yet, local funds remain unspent on such a budget line(s) – grantee should make an assessment of how much time is realistically available and whether it can carry out additional work on that budget line(s) insofar as it will increase the value of the project. Grantee should then submit a summary proposal note, to the DONOR, on how it expects to utilize such available funds, including the value it expects it will add to the project. Any such spending of available funds must not raise the spending on such a budget line above the original allocation in DONOR currency [Delete or amend this clause as appropriate]

8.4   Where the DONOR's currency performs weakly against Grantee currency, and as a result, less local currency becomes available for spending, the DONOR will NOT be increasing its funding commitment to make up for the difference [Delete or amend this clause as appropriate]

9. INTEREST & BANK CHARGES

9.1   If the Grantee keeps the DONOR funds in an interest-bearing account, the interest earned must be declared to DONOR in the financial reports. DONOR will determine and inform the Grantee in writing whether or not interest earned shall be added to the Grantee's project funds or returned to DONOR.

9.2   In the event that DONOR needs to make fund transfers to the Grantee as part of the fulfilment of this agreement (*and vice versa*), it is agreed that bank or other related transfer charges will be borne [fully by DONOR / individually by DONOR and the Grantee] [delete one as appropriate]

10. CASH FLOW / DISBURSEMENTS

10.1   DONOR will provide disbursed funds according to the following schedule:

[Enter here a fixed payment schedule table, complete with dates or periods of disbursement or a worded schedule to clearly indicate the timing of fund disbursements]

10.2   Payments will be made by bank transfer, payable to:

[Enter here the Grantee's Bank name, Account Name, Branch, Address, other IDs to which all transfers related to this project shall be made into]

Grantee's Bank Name: xxx
Bank Address: xxx
Account Name: xxx
Account Number: yyy
Account Currency: yyy
IBAN Number: yyy
SWIFT Number: zzz
BIC/ABA Number: zzz
Names of Signitories: zzz

Should any of the details above change, the Grantee must inform the DONOR immediately

10.3   Funds disbursed to the Grantee under this Agreement must be held in a bank account separate from other incomes. If however this is impractical and DONOR's funds must be held in a pool bank account, the Grantee must first provide a letter of assurance to the DONOR, that it has well-structured and functional accounting systems and controls to ensure incomes and expenditures relating to the specific project funded under this Agreement can be separately accounted for and reported on. [Delete or amend this clause as appropriate]

10.4   When requesting a disbursement of funds under this Agreement, you must use the form (or format) advised by the DONOR, ensuring a responsible officer in your organisation certifies the claim being made as truthful, complete and free from error. [Delete or amend this clause as appropriate]

10.5   If this Agreement is entered into on the understanding that the DONOR is funding part of the overall project cost and that co-financing will be sought to compliment the contributions committed under this Agreement, then it is a condition of the DONOR that additional funds for project in excess of the DONOR's commitment are in place prior to the commencement of each funding year. Any difficulties which arise in securing co-funding must be reported to the DONOR immediately.

10.6   In signing this Agreement, the Grantee declares that all co-founding:

   a. Is in place, at least for the first year of this project and at the commencement of each financial year subsequently. The Grantee, further commits that where it is unable to find co-financing as originally anticipated, it has and will without limit cover the same from its unrestricted reserves.

   b. Will not be committed to any other use other than those covered under this Agreement.

   c. Are funds unencumbered by any obligation to any third party to repay;

d. Are NOT derived from other funds originating from the DONOR whether directly or indirectly

Any difficulties that may arise with additional funding must be reported immediately to the DONOR

10.7 The Grantee is required to draw up and agree MoUs with all project partners who are administering project funding. Copies of the MoUs need to be retained for DONOR's viewing as the need may arise. These need to be in place prior to any transfer of funds to any partners. The MoU should include similar terms as included in the Agreement between DONOR and Grantee. It should include arrangements for financial accountability controls, funding received, developmental outcomes and value for money.

10.8 At the completion of the project / Agreement expiry, all funds held in hand by the Grantee must be returned immediately to the DONOR using the following bank details, no later than X days after the project end. The transfer must include as reference, the project's ID and the Grantee must inform the DONOR in writing (*e.g. email*) once the transfer has been completed, stating any references used in order to facilitate tracking of the same:

Donor's Bank Name:	xxx
Bank Address:	xxx
Account Name:	xxx
Account Number:	yyy
Account Currency:	yyy
IBAN Number:	yyy
SWIFT Number:	zzz
BIC/ABA Number:	zzz

11. APPROVAL OF EXPENSES

11.1   Expense reports should be presented using the same budget line descriptions as the agreed detailed budget.

11.2   All expense reports must be signed by the appropriate authority representing the Grantee and must contain the following declaration:

> *"I declare the expenses reported herein were made for the purposes agreed with DONOR, have not been and will not be reported to any other funding agency for the purposes of justifying the use of its funds or of requesting reimbursement. I also confirm that the expenses reported have been wholly and necessarily made in satisfying the sole objectives agreed with DONOR under this contract, are true and generally free from material error(s)"*

11.3   The Grantee's financial report will be analysed on the basis of incurred expenses that are reasonable, allowable and necessary in accordance with the terms and conditions of this grant.

- Reasonable costs shall mean costs that do not exceed those which would be incurred by an ordinarily prudent person in the conduct of normal business.
- Necessary costs shall mean those costs which are necessary for the execution of the grant and which have been approved.
- Allowable costs shall mean those costs which conform to any limitations set forth in this grant.
- Unallowable or disallowed costs, direct or indirect, include but are not limited to the following examples: Advertising, bad debts, legal fees, contingencies, entertainment, fines, penalties, interest, fundraising, losses on other awards, etc.

11.4   DONOR reserves the right to refuse to accept expense requests deemed inappropriate under this sub-grant, because of non-compliance with this agreement, including any conditions incorporated in this agreement by association, or contravention of the laws or accepted accounting practices by which DONOR abides. Where funds have been advanced to the Grantee, the Grantee will return such disallowed costs within XX working days after notice of disallowance from DONOR is issued. DONOR will take all appropriate steps to recover funds to the value of any unapproved expenses, including without limitation deducting any outstanding sum from further payments due from DONOR to the Grantee under this agreement.

12. MONITORING, REPORTING & RIGHTS OF ACCESS

12.1   Implementation or Progress reports will be provided to DONOR according to the following schedule:

#	REPORT TYPE	PERIOD COVERED	SUBMISSION DATE(S)	REPORTING FREQUENCY	NOTES

12.2   Audited Annual Accounts (AAA)

12.2.1   For each year covered by any part of the DONOR's funding, the Grantee shall submit an Audited Annual Accounts covering the Grantee's entire organisation, carried out by an independent, registered, external auditor of good standing. The submission includes any Management Letter issued by the Auditor, highlighting their findings on the internal controls, accounting controls and the general control environment. The AAA must be appropriately signed by the Grantee's Trustees or Board of Directors <u>and</u> certified by the auditors as being a true reflection of the Grantee's finances and general state for the period reviewed. [Delete or amend this clause as appropriate]

12.2.2   The AAA must clearly show DONOR's total grant disbursements to the Grantee for the period covered by the AAA, whether on the face of the Accounts or in its accompanying notes. Where the DONOR funds more than one project of the Grantee, the details of the DONOR's funding contributions in the AAA must reflect the exact amounts contributed to each separate activity of the Grantee, for the year under review. In the event that this depth of disclosure is impossible on the face of the AAA or its supporting notes, a separate statement, signed and certified by the Auditors, shall be issued, reconciling the separate funding contributions of the DONOR's to any bulk amount attributed to the DONOR in the AAA. [Delete or amend this clause as appropriate]

12.2.3   One copy of the AAA, bearing appropriate signatures, together with any additional Reconciliation Statements (*where necessary*) must be submitted to the DONOR as a scanned PDF document / in original hardcopy [Delete or amend this clause as appropriate], no later than X months after the Grantee's Financial Year end. The AAA submitted must under no circumstances, differ from that submitted to any Statutory body with similar requirements.

12.3   Annual Technical Reporting

12.3.1   Within X months from the date a final signature is appended to this Agreement, the Grantee shall submit a revised, up to date version Logical Framework (Logframe) including and where appropriate, baseline information. Where this revised Logframe is deemed acceptable to the DONOR, the same shall now form the reference document for project implementation, monitoring and evaluation. The opportunity exists, for the Grantee to request/suggest changes to the Logframe at the annual reporting stages. [Delete or amend this clause as appropriate]

12.3.2   The Grantee shall, without fail, submit a Technical progress report no later than X months, following the end of DONOR's financial / Calendar year end in the formats approved by the DONOR. [Delete or amend this clause as appropriate]. The report shall cover the period of the DONOR's financial / Calendar year. In the year that the Project comes to an end, it is permitted for the final Technical Report to be made up of the last fifteen (15) months. Where the difference between the last project year end and the project closure date is more than 15 months, separate annual and closure technical reports shall be produced and submitted accordingly. The Final project technical report must be submitted no later than X months, following the project/agreement expiry date. [Delete or amend this clause as appropriate].

12.3.3 At the end of the project, and in addition to the Final Technical Report high-lighted above, a Project Evaluation Report must be provided. The evaluation must be carried out by an external person, independent of the Grantee and should be carried out towards the end of the Agreement, preferably not after. This is to ensure that e.g. staff, whose employment contracts may not extend beyond the Agreement date but who are nonetheless crucial to the evaluation are at post to input into such an evaluation. The evaluation report MUST be submitted together with the Final Technical Report.

12.4   Annual Project Financial Reporting

12.4.1 Within X months from the date a final signature is appended to this Agreement, the Grantee shall have the option to submit a revised, up to date project budget including and where appropriate a quarterly disbursement forecast for the first year. Once acceptable to the DONOR, this revised and up to date Budget shall form the basis for project implementation, monitoring and evaluation. The opportunity exists, for the Grantee to request/suggest changes to the Project Budget at the annual reporting stages. [Delete or amend this clause as appropriate]

12.4.2 The Annual Financial Report (AFR) is NOT the same as the AAA. The AFR is concerned primarily with individual projects, covered by individual DONOR Agreements. Where the Grantee has more than one such funded project with the DONOR, each shall have a separate AFR requirement but all shall be covered in the same AAA.

12.4.3 The Grantee shall produce and submit an AFR covering DONOR's financial / Calendar year, no later than X months, following the end of DONOR's financial / Calendar year end, and in the format approved by the DONOR. In the AFR, the Grantee's actual expenditures for the year (or period under review) must be reported against the most recent detailed budget agreed by the DONOR. [Delete or amend this clause as appropriate]. In the year that the Project comes to an end, it is permitted for the final Project Financial Report to be made up of the last fifteen (15) months. Where the difference between the last project year-end and the project closure date is more than 15 months, separate annual and closure financial reports shall be produced and submitted accordingly.

The Final project financial report must be submitted no later than X months, following the project/agreement expiry date. **[Delete or amend this clause as appropriate]**.

12.4.4   Where a report is considered to be inadequate, resubmission will be required.

> ***It is essential the Grantee keeps DONOR informed of any significant changes to the project. Any such change, should be reported as soon as possible before year-end report dates.***

12.5   Rights of Access

12.5.1   DONOR reserves the right for its staff, or designated representatives, to gain access to this project's documentation and personnel, the sites of project implementation, as well as the office or storage premises where project funds or other resources are managed; and to request the views of third parties such as beneficiaries or community members, in order to verify project activities and outputs. This right continues for three years after the end date of this agreement or its termination, whichever is the earliest.

13. PROJECT EVALUATION

13.1   The Grantee's activities will be subject to a formal evaluation process, as follows:

#	EVALUATION TYPE	PERIOD COVERED	TIMING OF EXECUTION	REPORT TYPE DUE	NOTES

13.2   The Grantee agrees to participate in any formal evaluation process.

13.3   The cost of any external evaluator will borne by DONOR/ the Grantee as per provisions in the detailed budget agreed **[delete as appropriate]**

14. MUTUAL OBLIGATIONS

The parties will co-operate to comply with ALL requests and regulations relating to this Agreement. As a matter of contractual obligation, the Grantee is required to read and fully understand the contract terms and obligations of this Agreement and the DONOR, to ensure that any additional support needed by the Grantee in shaping that understanding is provided. The additional applicable parts of this Agreement have either been attached as Annexes or a link provided to their location, electronically. They should be read together with this Agreement before endorsing signatures.

15. FINANCIAL INTEGRITY & AUDIT

15.1   The Grantee agrees to ensure that an adequate system of internal control is maintained such that

DONOR can rely on the integrity and transparency of the financial reports issued by the Grantee. The Grantee further agrees as part of those internal controls, that any misappropriation, gross financial negligence and any other financial error involving amounts that exceed £xxx [please state appropriate threshold and currency here] shall be immediately notified to DONOR as soon as it becomes known.

15.2   The Grantee agrees to keep complete and accurate books of financial account and records relating to this Agreement.

15.2.1 DONOR/ the Grantee [delete as appropriate] will arrange for project audits to be conducted by an external auditor according to the following schedule:

#	TYPE OF AUDIT	PERIOD COVERED	TIMING OF EXECUTION	REPORT TYPE DUE

15.2.2   The auditor's costs will be paid for by the DONOR/Grantee, as allowed in the detailed budget [delete/ amend as appropriate]. DONOR must approve of the auditor, if selected by the Grantee. [delete or amend this clause as appropriate]

15.3   Audit reports, from audits organised by the Grantee shall be submitted to DONOR within 5 working days of such reports being issued by the auditor.

15.4   Any Final project audit should be completed and submitted within 60 days of this Agreement's end / Project completion date [delete or amend this clause as appropriate]

15.5   DONOR reserves the right to arrange for additional external audits at any time, as is deemed Necessary, at its discretion.

15.6   The Grantee agrees to provide full and open access for auditors *(whether DONOR staff, or their external representatives)* to its facilities, beneficiaries, books, records and staff, and to provide them with the information they require.

16. ORGANISATIONAL POLICIES

The Grantee agrees it will follow and be accountable for its own organisational policies, except where they contradict the terms of this Agreement.

16.1   No offer, payment, consideration or benefit of any kind, which constitutes an illegal act, fraud, theft, bribery or corrupt practice, shall be made – whether directly or indirectly – as an inducement or reward in relation to tendering, award, or execution of this Agreement. Any such practice will be grounds for the immediate termination of this Agreement and for such additional action, civil and/or criminal, as may be appropriate. At the discretion of DONOR, a further consequence of any such practice can be the definite exclusion from any further funding provided by DONOR.

The Grantee further agrees that it shall, as part of the conditions of the Agreement, put in place, a reasonably acceptable policy on *"Theft, Fraud, Bribery and Corruption"*; to disseminate the same to all its staff; and that it is accompanied by clear procedures for "Whistle-blowing" [delete this clause if not appropriate]

16.2   No employee, officer or agent of the Grantee, shall participate in the selection, award or the full/partial administration of a contract/activity supported by DONOR funds if a real conflict of interest is involved. This conflict of interest will also exist if the employee, officer or agent or any member of his/her family, his or her partner or an organization which employs or is about to employ any of the parties indicated herein, has a financial or other interest in the firm selected for an award. The employees, officers or agents of the Grantee shall neither solicit nor accept gratuities, favours or anything of monetary value from contractors or other parties relating to the delivery of this project.

16.3   DONOR insists on the highest standards of honesty and probity. We do not accept or condone fraud, theft, bribery or corruption irrespective of whether it is attempted internally by our employees or individuals within Grantee and other organizations associated in whatever way with the Grantee or DONOR. Members of Grantee and other organizations associated with DONOR and members of the public are encouraged to report evidence-based concerns about fraud, theft, bribery or corruption to the appointed senior officer of DONOR responsible for such matters.

16.4   The Senior Officer of the DONOR responsible for Whistleblowing issues can be contacted directly in any of the following ways: [delete this clause if not appropriate]

- By writing to the SO-Whistleblowing, DONOR Organization, ABC Street, City, Postcode, Country. Write **'Private and confidential'** on the envelope;
- By telephoning the confidential hotline on + 333 – 111 – 222 – 222. Voicemail messages can be left 24 hours a day;
- By sending an e-mail to SOwhistleblower@DONOR.org

17. PROCUREMENT, TITLES AND INTELLECTUAL PROPERTY

17.1   Procurement

17.1.1   Assets purchased by the Grantee with funds under this Agreement shall remain the property of:_____ [Please insert the appropriate name(s): ownership here]. The Grantee further agrees that for Capital (or Fixed Assets) purchased under this Agreement, it shall keep a full record, preferably a Fixed Assets Register of all fixed assets with purchase value of £500 or more and which should be submitted to the DONOR at the end of each financial year [Please enter the appropriate threshold and currency, and/or amend terms]

17.1.2   The Grantee agrees that all procurements:

- Shall be conducted within the scope of Generally Accepted Accounting Principles (GAAP);
- Are for the appropriate assets, materials or services solely necessary for the project's execution;
- Are of the correct quality, at an advantageous price, and that value for money considerations have been made in full;
- Are allowable as per all the terms in this Agreement and its associated Budget detail;
- And the processes engaged are fully transparent, documented and free from all conflicts of interest, fraud, bribery, illegality and corruption

Where the value of any single procurement exceeds £xx [*Please enter the appropriate threshold and currency, and/or amend terms*], the Grantee shall seek DONOR advice in the selection of a suitable supplier or where specified by the DONOR, shall use one appointed by the latter.

17.2   Disposal Procedures

17.2.1   Any disposal of assets shown on the inventory or otherwise held, will be subject to approval by the DONOR. On project completion, the Grantee shall submit to DONOR, a proposal of how each *(or a class of)* asset is to be disposed, including justifications on whether or not such assets be transferred to local partners for project continuity or other. Such a request must be responded to in writing by the DONOR before any actual disposal takes place. Such a disposal request must include justifications for why the disposal has become necessary, how the proceeds are intended to be utilized and what value such a treatment of proceeds will add to the project dlivery.

17.2.2 Where cash proceeds are recognized from a disposal, the Grantee shall consult with the DONOR and based on the latter's discretion, the proceeds may either be required to be returned back to the DONOR or spent on other budget lines, depending on timing and the additional value that may be added to the project by doing so.

17.3 Intellectual Property

17.3.1 Intellectual property rights covering all material produced in connection to the project funded under this Agreement, electronic or non-electronic, shall remain the property of the Grantee. [delete or amend this clause if not appropriate]

17.3.2 The Grantee further by this Agreement, assigns the DONOR an immediate and automatic worldwide, non-exclusive irrevocable and royalty-free licence to **use** all its intellectual works falling under 17.3.1 above. The term **"use"** shall mean, without restriction, the reproduction, publication and sub-licence of all the works and the intellectual property rights therein, anywhere in the world.

18. DISPUTE RESOLUTION

18.1 This Agreement is governed by the laws of _____ [Please insert the appropriate country jurisdiction]. The parties shall first try to resolve any disputes relating to this Agreement by the mutual agreement of the parties or by mediation. If the dispute is not so resolved, it shall be referred to an arbitrator who is acceptable to both parties or, failing that, to a team of three arbitrators, consisting of one chosen by each party and the third chosen by those two arbitrators.

18.2   Arbitration shall take place in _____ [Please insert
       the appropriate country/place name(s), language and where applicable, time
       lapse after the dispute arises]

18.3   The decision of the arbitrator(s) shall be final and binding on all parties.

19. TERMINATION

19.1   Either party may terminate this Agreement by giving X month [Insert the
       appropriate] prior written notice . Immediately upon receipt of the termina-
       tion notice, each party shall try to mitigate or avoid ongoing costs related to
       this Agreement.

19.2   Upon expiry or termination of this Agreement (based on the date of receipt
       of the termination *notice)*, DONOR shall stop all financial assistance to the
       Grantee without in any way becoming liable for any further costs; and the
       Grantee shall reimburse to DONOR all project funds, which have not been
       spent or which have been disbursed to the Grantee by DONOR, no more than
       within X month [Insert the appropriate] just prior to the termination notice
       being served, if so requested by DONOR, including but not limited to any disal-
       lowed costs. [Delete this clause if not appropriate]

19.3   The expiry or termination of this Agreement shall not affect any accrued rights
       or liabilities of either party, nor shall it affect the effectiveness of any provision
       of this Agreement, which is intended to become effective or to continue to be
       effective on or after expiry or termination. This clause shall remain in full force
       and effect notwithstanding any termination or expiry of this Agreement.

19.4   DONOR may terminate this Agreement, without giving any notice and with-
       out paying compensation of any kind, where the Grantee including Trustees,
       Directors, Senior Management and employees:

       a. Fail, without justification, to fulfil any of the obligations incumbent on
           the Grantee and, after being given notice by correspondence to comply
           with those obligations, still failed to do so or to furnish a satismfactory

explanation within X month [Insert the appropriate] of such a correspondence;

b. Is bankrupt, being wound up, is having its affairs administered by the court, has entered into an arrangement with creditors, has suspended business activities, is the subject of proceedings concerning these matters or is in any analogous situation arising from a similar procedure provided for in national or international legislation or regulations. The Grantee further agrees under this circumstances that any funds disbursed to it by DONOR within X month [Insert the appropriate] of its entering into any arrangement with creditors, shall have recovery preference above all other creditors on its Statement of Affairs (or accounting books) as at the date of cessation; [delete this clause if not appropriate]

c. Has been convicted of an offence concerning professional conduct by a judgement;

d. Engages in any act of theft, fraud, bribery or corruption or is involved in any criminal activity or any other illegal activity detrimental to the reputation or financial interest of DONOR;

e. Changes legal status, unless an addendum recording that fact is drawn up;

f. Makes false or incomplete statements to obtain the grant provided for in this Agreement or provides reports that do not reflect truth or reality;

g. Does not comply with the requirements of this Agreement

20. EMPLOYEES

Each party shall engage and be responsible for its own employees, their conduct, welfare and security, and for all salaries, taxes, benefits, insurances and social payments in respect of them.

21. INDEMNITIES

DONOR shall in no way be liable for the acts or defaults of the Grantee, its agents, employees or subcontractors. the Grantee shall indemnify and hold harmless, the DONOR against all liabilities, losses and expenses arising from or in connection with the activities of the Grantee, its agents, subcontractors or employees, including without limitation any liabilities, losses or expenses relating to their breach of this Agreement, negligence or intentional wrongdoing. [Delete this clause if not necessary]

22. CONFIDENTIALITY, COMMUNICATIONS AND VISIBILITY

22.1   Confidentiality Issues

A party may receive confidential information of the other party in connection with this Agreement.

Neither party shall disclose confidential information of the other to any person or third-party or use such confidential information for its own purposes without the owner's prior written consent. Despite this confidentiality requirement, nothing prevents the parties from fulfilling their obligations under this Agreement or complying with any governmental or judicial request relating to this Agreement. Confidential information means any information (written, oral or observed) relating to:

(a) donor and potential donors;
(b) beneficiaries;
(c) employees;
(d) business and strategic plans;
(e) finances; and
(f) relationship with any governmental or quasi-governmental entity.

Confidential information also includes information marked or otherwise designated "CONFIDENTIAL" by its owner or which the other party _knows or reasonably should know_ is not generally known to the public. Confidential information does not include information already publicly known or readily available from public sources. Each party shall take steps necessary to assure that its employees, agents and subcontractors comply with these obligations. [Delete or amend this clause if not necessary]

22.2 Recognition and Visibility

The Grantee will give reasonable and appropriate recognition to the DONOR's funding support in any media coverage of the project, whether local or international. The content of the recognition should first be discussed with the DONOR or its appointed representatives. The Grantee further agrees to support the DONOR with all necessary data about its project, that the latter needs, in formulating its own media content.

Unless otherwise stated by the DONOR, the Grantee shall, in all communications with the public or third parties about this project, employ also, the use of DONOR's logo or other specified artwork, except where it can be reasonably anticipated that such depictions or associations with DONOR, may increase the risks of loss to life, limb or property or any other loss that is reasonably disproportionate to such recognition.

23. AMENDMENTS

This Agreement states the parties' complete understanding, and no other discussions or documents are incorporated into or otherwise apply to this Agreement. The parties can only revise this Agreement in writing.

24. SIGNATURES:

Any additional guidelines, appendices and other documentations referred to in this Agreement are construed as forming an integral part of this entire Agreement. If the terms and conditions outlined in this and all inferred components to this Agreement are acceptable to [**Enter Grantee's Name Here**], this Agreement will become effective on the date of last signature.

Please sign and keep one original copy of this Agreement for your own records and send DONOR the other original signed copy.

a) *On behalf of International DONOR:*

Signature_____Date _____/_____/_____/

Name_____

Position _____

b) **On behalf of [*Grantee's name*]:**

Signature_____Date _____/_____/_____/

Name_____

Position _____

5.

MEMORANDUM OF UNDERSTANDING
WITH LOCAL PARTNERS

1. THE IDENTIFICATION

In order that it is clear that this contract is the one and the same referred to by all parties, it is herein stated the peculiar identification, by which this grant shall be identified by all parties:

The Identification of this Grant in the records of XYZ is: _____

Name of Primary Donor(s) for this contract is: _____

Donor's Reference ID(s) to which this sub-grant relates: _____

2. THE PARTIES

This Memorandum of Understanding *(MoU), (hereinafter referred to as "Agreement")* is between XYZ *(hereinafter referred to as "XYZ")*, [enter *address of XYZ* here] and or its country representation XiYiZi at [*address of XYZ local office*] and [*name and address of Partner*] *(hereinafter referred to as "Partner")*.

3. CONTEXT

[state here, the circumstances within which it became necessary for this project to be initiated]

4. VALIDITY PERIOD OF CONTRACT

This Agreement and hence the project (or activities) it relates to enters into force on [Enter contract start date] and expires on [Enter contract end date]

5. PROJECT DESCRIPTION

The purpose of this grant is to:

[Enter here, the summary purpose / objectives for which this grant is being awarded to the partner]

A Project Description [*or work-plan*] is attached as annex 1, and is incorporated into this Agreement. The grant purpose and Project Description are collectively referred to here as the "Project". They are considered to form an integral part of this Agreement. If this Agreement and the annexes contradict each other, the text of this Agreement should be used as the authoritative version.

6. GRANT FUNDING

XYZ agrees to provide, according to the payment schedule or budgets and other terms herein, up to a total not exceeding [*state TOTAL grant and donor currency*] to the Partner. The grant will amount to the local or other receiving currency amount achieved by converting this at the one or various time(s) of disbursement(s).

7. PROJECT BUDGET

The agreed detailed budget for this contract is attached as annex 2. Listed here only, are the main summaries of the same budget:

	Main Budget Titles	Budget Allocation
1	Fixed Assets	H 90,000
2	Personnel Costs	H 250,000
3	Monitoring & Evaluation	H 160,000
etc.	etc.	etc.
Total		

	Financial Year	**Amount Approved**
1	2014/15	H 125,000
2	2015/16	H 231,000
3	2016/17	H 144,000
etc.	etc	etc
Total		

8. PROJECT MODIFICATIONS / VARIATIONS

8.1   Variation of x% between main (or individual) budget lines is permitted without prior written permission from XYZ. Any variation exceeding x% must first be authorised by XYZ in writing.

8.2   XYZ will not be liable for any expenses incurred by the recipient in excess of the amounts shown in the budget (if has not been approved prior by XYZ)

8.3   XYZ will not pay or reimburse any expenses incurred relating to activities not included in the detailed budget or Project description, unless these have been authorised in advance by XYZ, in writing.

8.4   The partner is not authorised to contract or sub-grant to other organisations to undertake work or activities defined in the program description without prior written approval from XYZ.

8.5   By signing this agreement the partner attests that the activities and expenses covered by this agreement will not be funded by any other source than XYZ and that the funds allocated and disbursed for these budgeted expenses shall not be used to fund expenses related to other donor budgets, even if temporarily.

9. INTEREST & BANK CHARGES

9.1   If the partner keeps the XYZ funds in an interest-bearing account, the interest earned must be declared to XYZ in the financial reports. XYZ will determine and inform the partner in writing whether or not interest earned shall be added to the partner's project funds or returned to XYZ.

9.2   In the event that XYZ needs to make fund transfers to the partner as part of the fulfilment of this agreement (and vice versa), it is agreed that bank or other related transfer charges will be borne [fully by XYZ / individually by XYZ and the Partner] [delete one as appropriate]

10. CASH FLOW / DISBURSEMENTS

10.1   XYZ will provide funds according to the following schedule:

[Enter here a fixed payment schedule table, complete with dates or periods of disbursement / a similar payment schedule as with the primary donor / or a worded schedule to clearly indicate the timing of fund disbursements]

10.2   Payments will be made by bank transfer, payable to:

[Enter here the Bank name, Account Name, Branch, Address, other IDs to which all transfers related to this project shall be made into]

11. APPROVAL OF EXPENSES

11.2   Expense reports should be presented using the same budget line descriptions as the agreed detailed budget.

11.3   All expense reports must be signed by the appropriate authority representing the partner and must contain the following declaration:

> *"I declare the expenses reported herein were made for the purposes agreed with XYZ, have not been and will not be reported to any other funding agency for the purposes of justifying the use of its funds or of requesting reimbursement. I also confirm that the expenses reported have been wholly and necessarily made in satisfying the sole objectives agreed with XYZ under this contract"*

11.4   The partner's financial report will be analysed on the basis of incurred expenses that are reasonable, allowable and necessary in accordance with the terms and conditions of this grant.

- Reasonable costs shall mean costs that do not exceed those which would be incurred by an ordinarily prudent person in the conduct of normal business.
- Necessary costs shall mean those costs which are necessary for the execution of the grant and which have been approved.
- Allowable costs shall mean those costs which conform to any limitations set forth in this grant.
- Unallowable or disallowed costs, direct or indirect, include but are not limited to the following examples: Advertising, bad debts, legal fees, contingencies, entertainment, fines, penalties, interest, fundraising, losses on other awards, etc.

11.5   XYZ reserves the right to refuse to accept expense requests deemed inappropriate under this sub-grant, because of non-compliance with this agreement, including any conditions incorporated in this agreement by association, or contravention of the laws or accepted accounting practices by which XYZ abides. Where funds have been advanced to the partner, the partner will return such disallowed costs within 15 working days after notice of disallowance from XYZ. XYZ will take all appropriate steps to recover funds to the value of any unapproved expenses, including without limitation deducting any outstanding sum from further payments due from XYZ to the partner under this agreement.

12. MONITORING, REPORTING & RIGHTS OF ACCESS

12.1   Implementation or Progress reports will be provided to XYZ according to the following schedule:

#	REPORT TYPE	PERIOD COVERED	SUBMISSION DATE(S)	REPORTING FREQUENCY	NOTES

12.2   Implementation or progress reports will be submitted in the following format:

[State clearly here, whether the progress reports are to be submitted according to a specific format, what that format is, and whether one has been included in this MoU as an annex]

12.3   XYZ reserves the right for XYZ or its designated representative to gain access to project documentation and personnel, the sites of project implementation, as well as the office or storage premises where project funds or other resources are managed; and to request the views of third parties such as beneficiaries or community members, in order to verify project activities and outputs. This right continues for three years after the end date of this agreement or its termination, whichever is the earliest.

12.4   By this agreement, the rights of access stated in 12.3 above, shall fully extend without restriction to the donors of XYZ (*whose funds are directly related to this project*), their auditors and its designated representatives. This right continues for three years after the end date of this agreement or its termination, whichever is the earliest.

13. PROJECT EVALUATION

13.1   The Partner's activities will be subject to a formal evaluation process, as follows:

#	EVALUATION TYPE	PERIOD COVERED	TIMING OF EXECUTION	REPORT TYPE DUE	NOTES

13.2   The Partner agrees to participate in any formal evaluation process.

13.3   The cost of any external evaluator will borne by XYZ/ the Partner as per provisions in the detailed budget agreed [delete as appropriate]

14. DONOR OBLIGATIONS

The parties will co-operate to comply with requests and regulations of the Donor(s) relating to this Agreement. As a matter of contractual obligation, the Partner is required to read and fully understand the contract terms and obligations of the primary donor(s) to whom XYZ is bound contractually and which contract forms a basis of this MoU. The applicable parts of such primary donor contracts have been attached as Annex 3, and should be read together with this MoU before appending endorsing signatures.

Every term and condition XYZ is bound to in such primary donor contracts are now also binding on the Partner.

15. FINANCIAL INTEGRITY & AUDIT

15.1   The Partner agrees to ensure that an adequate system of internal control is maintained such that XYZ can rely on the integrity and transparency of the financial reports issued by the Partner. The Partner further agrees as part of those internal controls, that any misappropriation, gross financial negligence and any other financial error involving amounts that exceed Hxxx [please state appropriate threshold and currency here] shall be immediately notified to XYZ as soon as it becomes known.

15.2 The Partner agrees to keep complete and accurate books of financial account and records relating to this Agreement.

15.2.1 XYZ/ the Partner [delete as appropriate] will arrange for audits to be conducted by an external auditor according to the following schedule:

#	TYPE OF AUDIT	PERIOD COVERED	TIMING OF EXECUTION	REPORT TYPE DUE

15.2.2 The auditor's costs to be paid by XYZ/ the Partner, as allowed in the detailed budget [delete as appropriate]. XYZ must approve the auditor if selected by the Partner. [delete this clause if not appropriate]

15.3 Audit reports, from audits organised by the Partner shall be submitted to XYZ within 5 working days of such reports being issued by the auditor.

15.4 Any Final project audit should be completed and submitted within 60 days of the sub-grant completion date. [delete this clause if not appropriate]

15.5 XYZ reserves the right to arrange for additional external audits at any time, as it deems by its discretion, necessary.

15.6 The Partner agrees to provide full and open access for auditors (*whether XYZ staff, Primary Donor staff or both their externally hired representatives*) to its facilities, beneficiaries, books, records and staff, and to provide them with the information required.

16. ORGANISATIONAL POLICIES

The Partner agrees it will follow and be accountable for its own organisational policies, except where they contradict the terms of this Agreement, including any conditions incorporated in this Agreement by association from XYZ's primary donor contract.

16.1   No offer, payment, consideration or benefit of any kind, which constitutes an illegal, fraud, theft, bribery or corrupt practice, shall be made – whether directly or indirectly – as an inducement or reward in relation to tendering, award of this Agreement, or execution of this Agreement. Any such practice will be grounds for the immediate cancellation of this Agreement and for such additional action, civil and/or criminal, as may be appropriate. At the discretion of XYZ, a further consequence of any such practice can be the definite exclusion from any further funding provided by XYZ.

The Partner further agrees that it shall, as part of the conditions of the Agreement, put in place, a reasonably acceptable policy on "Theft, Fraud, Bribery and Corruption"; to disseminate the same to all its staff; and that it is accompanied by clear procedures for "Whistle-blowing" [delete this clause if not appropriate]

16.2   No employee, officer or agent of the Partner, shall participate in the selection, award or administration of a contract supported by XYZ funds if a real conflict of interest would be involved. This conflict of interest will also exist when the employee, officer or agent or any member of his family or immediate family, his or her Partner or an organization which employs or is about to employ any of the parties indicated herein, has a financial or other interest in the firm selected for an award. The employees, officers or agents of the Partner shall neither solicit nor accept gratuities, favours or anything of monetary value from contractors, or parties to sub-agreements.

6.3   XYZ insists on the highest standards of honesty and probity. We do not accept or condone fraud, theft, bribery or corruption irrespective of whether it is attempted internally by our employees or individuals within Partner and other organizations associated in whatever way with the Partner or XYZ. Members of Partner and other organizations associated with XYZ and members of the public are encouraged to report evidence-based concerns about fraud, theft or corruption to the appointed senior officer of XYZ responsible for such matters.

16.4   The Senior Officer of XYZ responsible for Whistleblowing issues can be contacted direct in any of the following ways: [delete this clause if not appropriate]

- By writing to the SO-Whistleblowing, XYZ Organization, ABC Street, City, Postcode, Country. Write **'Private and confidential'** on the envelope;
- By telephoning the confidential hotline on + 333 – 111 – 222 – 222. Voicemail messages can be left 24 hours a day;
- By sending an e-mail to SOwhistleblower@XYZ.org

17. TITLE TO PROPERTY AND INTELLECTUAL MATERIAL

17.1   Property purchased by the Partner with funds under this grant is the property of:_____ [Please insert the appropriate name(s) ownership here]. The Partner further agrees that for Capital (or Fixed Assets) purchased under this Agreement, it shall keep a full record, preferably a Fixed Assets Register of all Fixed Assets with purchase value of Hxxx or more [Please enter the appropriate threshold]

17.2   Written, creative, scientific, technological and any other work or intellectual asset, developed by the Partner as a direct consequence of this sub-grant remains the property of :_____ [Please insert the appropriate name(s) ownership here]

17.3   Written work developed by XYZ as a direct consequence of this sub-grant remains the property of XYZ.

18. DISPUTE RESOLUTION

18.1   This Agreement is governed by the laws of _____ [Please insert the appropriate country name(s)]. The parties shall first try to resolve any disputes relating to this Agreement by the mutual agreement of the parties or by mediation. If the dispute is not so resolved, it shall be referred to an arbitrator who is acceptable to both parties or, failing that, to a team of three arbitrators, consisting of one chosen by each party and the third chosen by those two arbitrators.

18.2   Arbitration shall take place in _____ [Please insert the appropriate country/place name(s), language and where applicable, time lapse after the dispute arises]

18.3   The decision of the arbitrator(s) shall be final and binding on all parties.

19. TERMINATION

19.1   Either party may terminate this Agreement by giving one (1) month's [Insert the appropriate] prior written notice . Immediately upon receipt of the termination notice, each party shall try to mitigate or avoid ongoing costs related to this Agreement.

19.2   Upon expiry or termination of this Agreement (*based on the date of receipt of the termination notice*), XYZ shall stop all financial assistance to the Partner without in any way becoming liable for any further costs; and the Partner shall reimburse to XYZ all project funds, which have not been spent or which have been disbursed to the Partner by XYZ, no more than within 3 months priorto termination notice being served, if so requested by XYZ, including without limitation any disallowed costs. [Delete this clause if not appropriate]

19.3   The expiry or termination of this Agreement shall not affect any accrued rights or liabilities of either party, nor shall it affect the effectiveness of any provision of this Agreement, which is intended to become effective or to continue to be effective on or after expiry or termination. This clause shall remain in full force and effect notwithstanding any termination or expiry of this Agreement.

19.4 XYZ may terminate the Contract, without giving any notice and without paying compensation of any kind, where the Partner including Trustees, Directors and Senior Management and employees:

   a. fails, without justification, to fulfil any of the obligations incumbent on the Partner and, after being given notice by correspondence to comply with those obligations, still fails to do so or to furnish a satisfactory explanation within one month of such a correspondence;

   b. is bankrupt or being wound up, is having its affairs administered by the court, has entered into an arrangement with creditors, has suspended business activities, is the subject of proceedings concerning those matter or is in any analogous situation arising from a similar procedure provided for in national legislation or regulations. The partner further agrees under this circumstances that any funds disbursed to it by XYZ within 6 months of its entering with any arrangement with creditors shall have recovery preference above all other creditors on its statement of affairs as at the date of cessation; [delete this clause if not appropriate]

   c. has been convicted of an offence concerning professional conduct by a judgement;

   d. engages in any act of theft, fraud, bribery or corruption or is involved in any criminal activity or any other illegal activity detrimental to the reputation or financial interest of XYZ;

   e. changes legal status, unless an addendum recording that fact is drawn up;

   f. makes false or incomplete statements to obtain the grant provided for in the Contract or provides reports that do not reflect reality;

   g. does not comply with requirements of this Contract.

20. EMPLOYEES

Each party shall engage and be responsible for its own employees, their conduct, welfare and security, and for all salaries, taxes, benefits, insurances and social payments in respect of them.

21. INDEMNITIES

XYZ shall in no way be liable for the acts or defaults of the Partner, its agents, employees or subcontractors. the Partner shall indemnify and hold harmless XYZ against all liabilities, losses and expenses arising from or in connection with the activities of the Partner, its agents, subcontractors or employees, including without limitation any liabilities, losses or expenses relating to their breach of this Agreement, negligence or intentional wrongdoing. [Delete this clause if not necessary]

22. CONFIDENTIAL INFORMATION

A party may receive confidential information of the other party in connection with this Agreement. Neither party shall disclose confidential information of the other to any person or third-party or use such confidential information for its own purposes without the owner's prior written consent. Despite this confidentiality requirement, nothing prevents the parties from fulfilling their obligations under this Agreement or complying with any governmental or judicial request relating to this Agreement. Confidential information means any information (written, oral or observed) relating to:

> (a) donors and potential donors;
> (b) beneficiaries;
> (c) employees;
> (d) business and strategic plans;
> (e) finances; and
> (f) relationship with any governmental or quasi-governmental entity.

Confidential information also includes information marked or otherwise designated "CONFIDENTIAL" by its owner or which the other party ***knows or reasonably should know*** is not generally known to the public. Confidential information does not include information already publicly known or readily available from public sources. Each party shall take steps necessary to assure that its employees, agents and subcontractors comply with these obligations.

23. AMENDMENTS

This Agreement states the parties' complete understanding, and no other discussions or documents are incorporated into or otherwise apply to this Agreement. The parties can only revise this Agreement in writing.

24. PROCUREMENTS

24.1   The Partner should ensure that any procurement using grant funds under this Agreement, adheres to international best practice and that it is transparent, fair and open. Where the Partner does not have the skills or capacity to carry out high value procurement, an XYZ approved procurement guideline, advice or agent should sought and used.

24.2   The Partner will establish and maintain an inventory of all items purchased above the value of Hxxx [Please enter the appropriate threshold]. An up to date inventory must be submitted to XYZ on at least an annual basis.

24.3   The Partner will be accountable to XYZ for the appropriate use and control of this inventory, in line with project objectives. Ultimate ownership of this inventory will remain with XYZ and any ownership transfer, after project completion, will be decided in writing by all parties.

25. COMMUNICATION AND BRANDING

25.1   The Partner will collaborate with XYZ and proactively look for ways to build support for development and raise awareness of XYZ's /Primary Donor funding [Please delete as appropriate]. The Partner will explicitly acknowledge XYZ's /Primary Donor [Please delete as appropriate] funding, in written and verbal communications about activities related to the Agreement, to the public or third parties, including in announcements, and through use, where appropriate, of XYZ's/Primary Donor's logo, unless otherwise agreed in advance by XYZ and in all cases subject to security and safety considerations of the Partner.

25.2   The Partner may use the XYZ's /Primary Donor logo [Please delete as appropriate] in conjunction with other donor(s) logos, and where the number of donors to a programme or project is such as to make co-branding impractical, acknowledgement of funding from XYZ's /Primary Donor [Please delete as appropriate] should be equal to that of other co-donors making contributions of equivalent amounts to the programme or project.

SIGNED:

a) *On behalf of International XYZ:*

Signature_____Date _____/_____/_____/

Name_____

Position_____

b) On behalf of [*Partner's name*]:

Signature_____Date _____/_____/_____/

Name_____

Position_____

6.

PROPOSAL BUDGET REVIEW CHECKLIST

INTRODUCTION

Many times, in a hurry to put together a project proposal for funding, we tend to be pressured for time and as such, lose the opportunity to carry out thorough reviews of the budgets accompnying the technical proposal(*s*). It is often sadly the case, we realise late, after donors' have approved technical and budget submissions that we remembered this or that expenditure may have been omitted, underbudgeted, or included in the wrong sections.

The purpose of this simple but useful checklist, is to enable anyone submitting a budget (*with a proposal*) to have an opportunity (*no matter how tight the deadline*) to review the supporting budget by asking a few very pertinent questions, hence reducing the risk of submitting a wrong budget.

SOME BUDGETING GOOD-PARCTICES

The Budgeting Process

The process of preparing a meaningful and useful budget is best undertaken as an organised and structured group exercise. The budget process involves asking a number of questions. These start with project plans and goals, **NOT** numbers. These questions can only be best answered by programme staff and with support from programme funding and finance staff working together:

- What are the objectives of the project?
- What activities will be involved in achieving these objectives?
- What resources will be needed to perform these activities?
- What will these resources cost? Do we have real measures e.g. from current projects?
- Where will the funds come from if donors cant support 100%?
- Is the expected result realistic?

Good Practice in Budgeting

Clarity

Since many different people will need to use the budget for different purposes, they should be able to pick it up and understand it without any additional explanation. Clarity and accuracy is crucial, particularly if staff of XYZ are likely to change during the life of a project *(which is normal to expect)*. So it is important to keep notes on all budgeting assumptions and how calculations have been made.

Timetable

There are several stages involved in constructing a budget before it can be submitted for approval to the donor/government body. It is a good idea to prepare a budgeting timetable and start the process early. This could be up to 2-4 weeks before the start of the draft submission, depending on the size of your project and the approach you plan to take. The usual *(though not entirely proper)* approach is to wait till project proposals are completed, then, as a result devote very little or no time at all to the actual budgeting process. It is rather advised, that the budget preparation process starts the same time as the technical proposal is being put together – e.g. there are some costs e.g. unit costs that can be collated without having to wait for the completion of the technical proposal

Estimating Costs & Notes

It is important to be able to justify your calculations when you are estimating costs. Even if you use the incremental method of budgeting, do not be tempted to simply take last year's budget and add a percentage amount on top for inflation. You should also think about whether all the costs are justified.

The 'Notes' section is particularly important. It explains to other people, how you have worked out your budget. This can really help them when they have to use the budget, or for instance to take account of changes in project plans or costs. It also helps the process when you are not available to give explanations. Other than that, notes can also be helpful to the project person him/herself when at a latter date you wish to remind yourself of "how" you arrived at certain figures *(bear in mind we can't always remember the basis upon which details of every budget line was created)*.

Contingencies

Try to avoid the practice of adding a 'bottom line' percentage for so-called 'contingencies' on the overall budget. As a rule, donors do not like to see this and it is not a very accurate way of calculating a budget; unless a donor specifically allows it. It is better to calculate and include a contingency amount for relevant items in the budget – e.g. salaries, insurance, and fuel to the extent that you justifiably anticipate that contingency to happen. Every item in your budget must be justifiable – adding a percentage on the bottom is difficult to justify – and difficult to monitor. If contingencies are at all justifiable, you will find out that they can be justified on the individual budget lines already included in the earlier sections of the budget.

Forgotten costs

Many a failed project is based on an under-costed budget. There is a tendency to under-estimate the true costs of running a project for fear of not getting the project funded. The most common of the forgotten costs are the indirect or non-project costs. Here are some of the most often overlooked costs:

- Staff related costs *(e.g. recruitment costs, training, benefits and statutory payments due on termination of contract or at end of the project)*
- Start-up costs *(e.g. publicity, office set up, statutory registration, legal and accountant fees, bank opening etc)*
- Vehicle running costs
- Equipment maintenance *(e.g. for photocopiers and computers)*
- Audit fees

Donor Requirements

Many delays in project approvals arise from the "to-and-fro" negotiations that carry on after the initial proposal submission. A lot of this centre around what the donor is willing to fund from the proposed budget. It is interesting to note however that the basis of such willingness is not discretionary but rather based on their general procedures, rules, standard regulations, etc. If the proposal is going to a donor that has been applied to before, it is worth reading a copy of previous grant contracts and regulations *(as these will normally tend to be standardized and will minimize the number of wrongs in the current proposal by hinting clearly on what is and not acceptable to that donor)*. If on the contrary this is a proposal to a new donor, it is worth looking at the donor's website or its application guidelines, as they would usually have on it documents covering the grant management and/or accounting reporting etc procedures or indeed in a lot of cases, even the entire proposal process *(which includes what is and is not acceptable for funding)*.

Programme:	
Donor:	
Project:	
Grant Amount:	
XYZ's Project Person:	
Donor Contact:	
Submission Deadlines:	
Specific Submission Requirements:	

This checklist is intended to assist in reviewing a proposed grant budget. It is not intended to provide complete instructions on preparing budgets, nor is it intended to provide donor specific guidelines – it cannot include all possible considerations.

Item	Comments	
A. Basic Budget Considerations		
1) Has the correct XYZ budgeting template been *used (e.g. a standard one exists within the XYZ organization)*		
2) Does the budget add up correctly both across and down?		
3) Do the expenses make sense for the type of program proposed? *(e.g. minefield disposal expert or architect's fees are not included for a straightforward borehole drilling project in a clear farming community?)*		
4) Is the budget consistent with the project timeline? *(e.g. do staff salaries cover 2 years for a 2-year project? In some countries a 13th month is paid)*		

Item	Comments	
5) Is the budget currency clearly indicated and is it in the Donor specified currency? (*Budgeting and grant award currencies may differ*)		
6) If the budget is multi-year, was a reasonable increase in unit cost (*especially for salaries*) budgeted over each year, to cover the likelihood of inflation?		
B. Budget Structure & Layout		
1) Does the donor require a specific budget format and was this format used? (*e.g. DFID, USAID, ECHO*). If this format is different from XYZ format, can they been linked with keys or specific accounting codes?		
2) Are there specific instructions in the Request for Proposals (RFP) that guide the budget format? (*Often true for many donor such EC, USAID*)		
3) Has a budget narrative (*or Notes*) been prepared if one was required? Is it consistent with the budget amounts?		
4) Are the line items described in the budget broad enough to reflect all expenses that will be charged to that budget line? (*e.g. Use the term "Office Occupancy" rather than "Office Rent" if the line item is meant to include rent, utilities, maintenance, etc.*)		
C. Equitable Share of General Costs		
1) Does the budget reflect a fully-costed project? A fully-costed project is one that bears its ***fair share*** of ALL necessary general country office and management and support expenses of HQ. (*i.e. are all necessary XYZ country & HQ office expenditure line items included?*)		
2) Are the percentages of shared costs reasonable for the project size? (*Regardless of coverage in other budgets, a project should bear a reasonable proportional amount of shared costs*)		
3) Review costs in light of the social, political and security status of the location. Are related costs, such as security guards, cash transfer fees, insurance etc included?		

Item	Comments	
D. Staffing Expenses		
1) Is the level of staffing reasonable for the project? (*This will include interns & temp staff etc.*) Is there value for money between staff qualifications sought and amounts to be remunerated?		
2) If needed, has the involvement of XYZ's Senior Officers been budget for?		
3) If support staff will be needed, have they been adequately covered for? Both in-country offices & for XYZ HQ in general. (*Consider involvement of Finance, Facilities, IT, HR, & other support staff*)		
4) If Country/regional/sub-offices of XYZ are part of project implementation, are their staff and administrative expenses budgeted for?		
5) Are salary scales reasonable compared to the industry and project environment? Are annual increases included if the budget is multi-year?		
6) Have staff costs been calculated at organizationally agreed rates (*e.g Employer National Insurance, other statutory costs, 13th month pay*)		
E. Other Staff-Related Expenses		
1) Review the current national staff benefit policy to ensure that all national staff benefits have been included		
2) Review if there is need for recruitment and training costs?		
F. Consultant Costs		
1) As required by projects, have adequate number of consultants and/or researchers been budgeted for? (*can they be sourced locally or regionally?*)		
2) In addition to fees payable, have all other associated costs i.e. travel, accommodation, per diem, honorarium etc. been included in the budget?		

Item	Comments	
G. Information & Dissemination		
1) If dissemination is required by project, have printing, design, radios, advert spaces, banners, documentaries, videos, websites costs been budgeted for?		
2) Have all associated costs such as lay-outs, peer review, proof reading, copying, editing, translation, launching etc been included in the budget?		
H. Donor/Statutory/Management/Evaluation Reporting		
1) If a grant requires an audit, have appropriate costs been budgeted?		
2) In case of XYZ overseas offices, if local government/statutory audits are required, was this included in addition to the specific grant audits?		
3) If project evaluation is part of the project implementation, then have reasonable costs been budgeted? *(e.g. cost of an local or external evaluator, travel, accommodation, per-diem, reporting/ printing)*		
I. Workshops, Meeting, Seminars etc		
1) Are meetings, seminars & workshops in project design, if yes, is there appropriate costs budgeted? *(e.g. logistics, materials & consumables, hospitality – food & tea, conference hall, travel costs for participants if any, professional fee for facilitators, translators etc.)*		
J. Accommodation and Travel		
1) Have trips for XYZ HQ personnel or visits to XYZ HQ included?		
2) Was consultant travel included if consultants are budgeted?		
3) Do trip expenses include both airfare and other travel expenses *(lodging, per-diem, visas, local transportation, vaccination, hospitality etc.)?*		

Item	Comments	
K. Fixed Assets or Capital Equipment		
1) Is the amount of furniture & equipment consistent with staffing levels and need of organization (XYZ-HQ & overseas + Local Partners)? *(e.g. are enough computers, phones, copiers/fax, generators, furniture etc. included, given staff levels and project needs?)*		
2) As per donor guidelines, are all capital or fixed asset items separated from non-capital items to facilitate reporting on?		
3) Is there a vehicle budgeted? If not, have relevant costs been budgeted for vehicle rental, fuel, local travel etc ?		
L. Other Costs		
1) Are vehicle budget lines *(rental, fuel, maintenance, insurance etc)* based on a consistent number of vehicles? – Particularly for XYZ overseas offices		
2) Have office rent, maintenance and utilities been included as separate line items? Particularly for XYZ overseas offices?		
3) Have all applicable types of communications costs been included? *(e.g. general communication expenses, mobile phone service, satellite phone service, internet, etc.)* ? Particularly for XYZ overseas offices		
4) Was equipment maintenance included? - Also for overseas XYZ offices		
5) If required by donor, was sufficient visibility costs budgeted? E.g. Logos, embossment costs, Press conferences, Interviews, etc?		
6) Was XYZ HQ insurance costs included? *(e.g. Terrorism Insurance)*		
7) Were banking charges or cash handling fees included?		
M. Local Partner(s)		
1) Are sub-grants shown as separate budget line items?		
2) If estimates were used in local currency, was a reasonable exchange rate used? Has a margin been factored in, for reasonable currency fluctuations?		

Item	Comments	
3) Do the sub-grantee budgets include indirect costs? *(Sub-grantee budgets may include indirect costs ONLY if the sub-grantee has an approved NICRA in case of US Grants. Ensure it is OK with other donors)*		
N. Overhead & Indirect Costs		
1) Have appropriate administrative overheads been budgeted for, using current XYZ overhead recovery rates and in line with donor regulations? 2) If all overheads at XYZ rates are not recoverable, are there other XYZ HQ costs that are acceptable for inclusion by the donor as separate budget lines?		
O. Co-financing		
1) Is co-financing actually required by the Request for Proposals (RFP) or in donor correspondence? Has it been secured or available from reserves? If not, co-financing should be avoided as it carries real financial commitment. Instead describe how funds will be leveraged in the proposal only.		

I/we acknowledge that I/we have reviewed and completed checklist after due consideration of donor and XYZ guidelines and generally accepted principles for this proposal.

Signature: ______________________ **Signature:** ______________________

Project Owner's Name: ______________________ **Peer Reviewer's Name:** ______________________

Designation: ______________________ **Designation:** ______________________

Date: ______________________ **Date:** ______________________

7.

SAMPLE ANTI FRAUD, BRIBERY,
THEFT & CORRUPTION POLICY & A
WHISTLEBLOWING POLICY

POLICY STATEMENT

XYZ, as an organization, insists on the highest standards of honesty and probity. We do not accept or condone fraud, theft, bribery or corruption irrespective of whether it is attempted internally by our employees or individuals within partner and other organizations associated in whatever way with XYZ. This Policy covers practices which are illegal and should be taken as confirmation of our stance on these matters.

We are committed to preventing fraud, theft, bribery and corruption through consistent application of robust control measures and also to ensuring that our culture is one of honesty, trust and opposition to fraud, theft, bribery and corruption. We expect and require that all individuals and organizations associated in whatever way with XYZ, will act with integrity; and that our staff at all levels will lead by example in these matters. Nevertheless, we recognize that controls cannot always deter those individuals who are determined to act without integrity. Therefore, our Whistle Blowing Policy positively encourages our staff and others to raise responsibly, any evidence-based concerns about fraud, theft, bribery and corruption that they may have in relation to XYZ and its work. These concerns may be about members of staff, or people who work with and for XYZ in other capacities (*our Donors, Service Providers, Suppliers or people who provide services to the public on our behalf*).

We are equally committed to ensuring that evidence-based concerns can be raised responsibly by individuals within partner and other organizations associated with XYZ and by members of the public in the knowledge that they will be treated in confidence and properly investigated.

THE 6 GUIDING PRINCIPLES

The 6 guiding principles that inform this policy are adapted from the UK's Ministry of Justice guidance:

Principle 1 – Proportionate procedures
XYZ's procedures to prevent theft, bribery and corruption by persons associated with it are proportionate to the fraud, bribery, theft and corruption risks it faces and to the nature, scale and complexity of its activities. They'll also be effectively enforced.

Principle 2 – Top-level commitment

Senior management of XYZ (including trustees) is committed to preventing fraud, bribery, theft and corruption by persons associated with it. They foster a culture within the organization in which fraud, bribery, theft and corruption is never acceptable.

Principle 3 – Risk assessment

XYZ assesses the nature and extent of its exposure to potential external and internal risks of fraud, bribery, theft and corruption by persons associated with it. The assessment is periodic, informed and documented.

Principle 4 – Due diligence

XYZ applies due diligence procedures, taking a proportionate and risk based approach, in respect of persons who perform or will perform services for or on its behalf, in order to mitigate identified fraud, bribery, theft and corruption risks.

Principle 5 – Communication (including training)

XYZ ensures that its fraud, bribery, theft and corruption prevention policies and procedures are embedded and understood throughout the organisation via internal and external communication, and training, that is proportionate to the risks it faces.

Principle 6 – Monitoring and review

XYZ monitors and reviews procedures designed to prevent fraud, bribery, theft and corruption by persons associated with it and makes improvements where necessary.

REASONS FOR THIS POLICY

Good Governance requires that XYZ clearly demonstrates that it:-

- Is firmly committed to dealing with fraud, bribery, theft and corruption;
- Will deal equally with perpetrators from inside (employees) and outside (Service Providers, partners, etc);
- Will draw no distinction, either in investigation or action, between cases that generate financial benefits and those that do not.

XYZ's Anti Fraud, Theft and Bribery and corruption Policy and the Whistle Blowing Policy both aim to prevent any attempted fraudulent or corrupt act, to set out the actions taken to prevent occurrence and, in the event that anything irregular should happen, the actions to be taken.

The policies are designed to:

- encourage prevention;
- promote detection;
- ensure protection;
- identify a clear approach for investigation; and
- where necessary, enforce prosecution or applicable penalty accordingly.

They endeavor to ensure:

- the consistent treatment of information regarding fraud, theft and bribery and corruption;
- compliance with necessary legislations and best practice;
- the routing of all enquiries through XYZ's Single Point of Contact (SPoC)'s Senior Officer (SO);
- proper investigation by the appropriate officer(s); and
- proper implementation of a fraud response plan.

DEFINITION OF SOME TERMS USED

Anti- is defined as the measures taken within XYZ to prevent, detect and investigate (instances of fraud, theft and bribery and corruption).

Fraud is defined as any deliberate act taken by one or more individuals to deceive or mislead with the objective of misappropriating assets or monies. It also covers financial reports or underlying records being distorted in an attempt to disguise fraudulent activity.

Theft is defined as illicitly taking assets from XYZ administration or related projects.

Bribery means offering, promising or giving someone a financial or other advantage to encourage them to perform their functions or activities improperly. It also means asking for or agreeing to accept a bribe. A bribe will remain a bribe irrespective of its cultural setting.

Corruption is defined as being the use of bribery, fraud or the irregular alteration and or distortion of records, to conceal and/or misappropriate assets of XYZ.

Whistle-blowing means, action by any individual or organisation to disclose malpractice. Refer to the Whistle Blowing Policy

SPoC or SO (Single Point of Contact, or Senior Officer) is the person authorized within XYZ to access telecommunications data, such as land-line, mobile networks, internet and e-mail data either directly or through professionals or other personnel that he/she may so choose to carry out such an assigned duty.

WHAT DO WE DO TO PREVENT FRAUD, THEFT, BRIBERY AND CORRUPTION?

Framework
The Management of XYZ, is responsible for implementing practical measures to ensure good governance and for monitoring the effectiveness of the same.

There are also a different degrees of external scrutiny of XYZ's operations by various bodies, including:

- The Government;
- Independent External Auditors;
- International contributing and non-contributing Donors.

Systems

XYZ is committed to implementing systems and procedures that incorporate efficient and effective internal controls. Our managers are responsible for ensuring these controls are effective, understood and observed, properly maintained and documented. XYZ has a mix of documented and other inferred codes of conduct expected of all those who work with and for XYZ.

Staff

We recognize that a key preventative measure in the fight against fraud, theft, bribery and corruption is to take effective steps at the recruitment stage to establish, as far as possible, the honesty and integrity of potential staff *(both permanent and temporary)*. Recruitment is therefore conducted in accordance with fair, rigid and thorough selection procedures and policies. We require all staff to comply with our policies, to follow XYZ's Codes of Conduct *(whether written or verbal)*.

Assessments

Carrying out a risk assessments – this should highlight specific areas where the risk, probability and possibility of fraud, bribery, theft and corruption is prevalent. It will allow XYZ to consider and mitigate such risks using its internal controls.

Accurate Accounting

Bribery and corruption often involves inaccurate financial record keeping. While good accounting policy and practice may not prevent bribery and corruption, it at least reduces the possibility for it to take place.

Gifts, entertainment and hospitality

These should be treated with caution. Such tokens of appreciation may be unavoidable and indeed desirable in building good relationships. However, a judgment on reasonableness, frequency and content must be made in each situation. Where there is uncertainty on appropriateness, it is better to err on the side of caution.

DETECTION AND INVESTIGATION

There are preventative systems, particularly internal control systems within XYZ, which are designed to provide indicators of any fraudulent activity. Generally these should be sufficient in themselves to deter fraud, however, XYZ's observant staff, its partners and members of the public may nevertheless become aware of fraud, theft, bribery or corruption. The Whistle-Blowing Policy provides more information about what you should do in such cases and how you can let us know.

DISSEMINATION

We recognize that the effectiveness of our Anti-Fraud, Theft, Bribery and corruption Policy will require us to disseminate all relevant policies to staff throughout the organisation and in most cases to our partners. To facilitate this, our staff is required to read and familiarize themselves with the contents of all our policies in this regards and with respect to our service partners, assess and agree to abide by the same in the execution of all projects related to XYZ.

RESPONSIBILITIES

Every employee of XYZ and all those closely associated with it in any form of operational relationship is individually responsible for:

- Acting with propriety at all times and in particular in the use of assets and finances of XYZ;
- Conducting themselves with integrity, objectivity, accountability, openness and honesty;
- Being alert to possibility that unusual behaviors or transactions could indicate bribery;
- Seeking advice from XYZ's Senior Officers if unsure about what acts are bribery or corruption;
- Reporting immediately to XYZ's Senior Officers, if they suspect bribery is/has taken place;
- Cooperating fully with whoever is conducting internal checks, reviews or investigations.

While any suspicious circumstances should be reported, employees and associated persons are required particularly to report on:

- The involvement of close family, personal or business ties with a prospective agent, representative or joint-venture partner or government that XYZ is soon to get involved with;
- Any history of fraud, bribery, theft and corruption in the country, organization, or by a person with which XYZ is engaging in business;
- Unusual requests for cash payments in the course of working for XYZ;
- Requests for unusual payment arrangements, for example via a third party;
- Requests for reimbursements of unsubstantiated or unusual expenses; or
- A lack of standard invoices and proper financial practices.

WHAT WILL XYZ DO IF FRAUD, THEFT, BRIBERY AND CORRUPTION IS REPORTED?

XYZ is committed to being robust in dealing with financial irregularity or malpractice and its management will deal swiftly and firmly with those who defraud or steal from XYZ or who are corrupt in direct and indirect businesses of XYZ. The SO is responsible for following up any allegation of fraud, bribery, theft or corruption and will inform the XYZ Team Leader or Directorship. In cases where allegations of fraud or bribery and corruption are found to be substantiated and in itself, substantive enough to affect the office or project's operations. The contributing donors and (or) the government will also be informed.

The investigating officer, usually the SO, will:

- deal promptly with the matter or complaint(s);
- record all evidence, ensure it is sound and adequately supported;
- ensure the security of all evidence;
- notify and liaise with the Team leader or Directorship where appropriate;
- investigate the evidence and/or contact and liaise with other agencies, e.g. the Police as needed.

Depending upon the nature and anticipated extent of the allegations, the SO will normally work closely with the rest of the XYZ Management Team and other agencies such as the police to ensure that all allegations and evidence are properly investigated and acted upon. XYZ will normally involve the police where financial impropriety is discovered to ensure that perpetrators are dealt with in accordance with the law.

POSSIBLE PENALTIES FOR FRAUD, THEFT, BRIBERY AND CORRUPTION

The potential penalties for anyone engaging in fraud, theft, bribery and corruption, include the following:

- Disciplinary actions and possible dismissal from XYZ or other related body
- Conviction under statutory national or international laws
- Limited or unlimited fines
- Debarring of an involved organization or person from future contracting
- Prison sentences of up to unspecified number of years

WHISTLE-BLOWING POLICY

INTRODUCTION

This section of the overall policy has been developed to provide guidance for employees and other stakeholders of XYZ on how to raise genuine concerns about malpractice in conduct on the part of individuals within XYZ, Service partners and other organisations associated in whatever way with XYZ. While the term *"whistle-blowing"* normally implies an internal process, staff of partner and other organisations associated with XYZ, and members of the public are equally encouraged to report evidence-based concerns about malpractice in conduct. Examples of malpractice in conduct include fraud, theft, bribery and corruption and other criminal activity; failure to comply with any legal or implied human duty; miscarriages of justice; danger to health and safety or the environment, and any attempt to cover up these issues.

POLICY STATEMENT

We have produced this Whistle-Blowing Policy to help XYZ staff and individuals outside XYZ to contact us with their concerns about malpractice in conduct. We are committed to being open, honest and accountable and to conducting our business with the highest standards of integrity and we expect our employees and individuals within partner and other organisations associated in whatever way with XYZ to maintain the same standards in everything they do. This policy aims to ensure that if you want to raise any serious concern, you can do so with confidence and without having to worry about being victimized, discriminated against or disadvantaged in any way as a result.

WHAT TYPES OF ACTION ARE COVERED BY THIS POLICY?

This policy is intended to deal with serious or sensitive concerns about wrongdoing, in the locations where XYZ operates, including the following:

- Criminal offences;
- Fraud, theft or bribery and corruption;
- Unauthorized use of resources owned by XYZ or any of its contractors;
- Unlawful acts;
- Health and safety infringements;
- Abuse of position for any unauthorized reason or for personal gain;
- Deliberate disregard for XYZ policies or any law or regulation of a significant nature;
- Professional misconduct;
- Discrimination against (a) persons because of their race, color, religion, ethnic or national origin, disability, age, sex, sexuality or class.

Your concern may be about members of staff, people who work directly for XYZ, Service Providers, partners, or people who provide services to the public on our behalf either in the UK or in the countries where we operate.

WHAT IS NOT COVERED?

This policy cannot be invoked to deal with serious or sensitive matters that are not directly traceable to XYZ's activities, or over which the Government in the respective country has a direct involvement with and which falls under their jurisdiction.

PROTECTING YOU

If the whistleblower's allegation is true and/or made in good faith, s/he has nothing to fear. XYZ understands that deciding to blow the whistle is not easy and XYZ will do its utmost to protect a whistleblower from any harassment, victimization or bullying. XYZ will keep whistleblower's concerns confidential if this is what is requested. In this case their names or other identities will not be revealed without express permission, unless it so has to be done to comply with the law. The SO will explain this at the time concern is raised so a whistleblower can decide whether or not to proceed. If the whistleblower works for XYZ, s/he should also know that any allegation made will not influence, or be influenced by, any unrelated disciplinary action against the whistleblower or any redundancy procedures that may affect her/him.

ANONYMOUS ALLEGATIONS

Because we will protect whistleblowers, we encourage them to give their name when an allegation is made. Concerns raised anonymously tend to be far less effective and if, for example, we do not have enough information, we may not be able to investigate the matter at all. If a whistleblower feels that s/he cannot give their name, we will decide whether or not to consider the matter. This will depend on:

- The seriousness of the matter;
- Whether the whistleblower's concern is credible; and
- Whether we can carry out an investigation based on the information we have been provided.

MALICIOUS ALLEGATIONS

If a whistleblower makes an allegation which s/he believes is true, but turns out to be unconfirmed by our investigation, we will not take any action against her/him. However, if the whistleblower makes a malicious allegation which they knew to have been untrue, we will take appropriate disciplinary or legal action against them.

HOW TO RAISE A CONCERN

Staff members may discuss the matter with the SO or their line manager, or they may wish to report the concern in any of the ways below.

Individuals outside XYZ are also encouraged to report all suspected irregularities, including suspected fraud, theft, or bribery and corruption to the SO. A confidential phone line and email address exist to receive calls and emails relating to suspected malpractice in the event that any member of public wishes to report anything suspicious.

You can contact the SO direct in any of the following ways:

- By writing to the **The Senior Officer - Reporting, P. O. Box 123, Town, XYZ.** Write **'Private and confidential'** on your envelope;
- By telephoning the **confidential hotline on 1234567890**. You can leave a voicemail message 24 hours a day. Only the SO can pick up the messages left;
- By sending an e-mail to **whistleblower@XYZ.com**

It is best for the whistleblower to put all concerns in writing and give the SO as much information as possible - including any relevant names, dates, places and so on. The earlier concerns are raised, the easier it is to take effective action.

HOW WE RESPOND TO YOUR CONCERNS

The way we deal with the concern will depend on what it involves. We will first make enquiries to decide whether we should carry out an investigation and, if so, how we should go about it. The concern raised may be investigated by the SO (our assigned officer), it may be dealt with, through our disciplinary process, or be referred to:

- The police
- Our external auditor; or
- An independent investigator

If the concern or allegation can be handled under any other procedure or policy, we will pass it on to the relevant person and let the whistleblower know. If we need to take urgent action, we will do this before carrying out any investigation.

The amount of contact a whistleblower will have with our assigned officer will depend on the nature of the concern, the potential difficulties involved, and how clear the information given us is. If the whistleblower needs to have a meeting, s/he can be accompanied by a friend, colleague or manager in whom s/he has confidence and who understands clearly the need for utter confidentiality. Meetings with the assigned officer will normally take place in our offices but can also be arranged elsewhere for neutrality. We will take steps to reduce any difficulties the whistleblower may experience as a result of raising a concern.

THE OFFICER RESPONSIBLE FOR THIS WHISTLE BLOWING POLICY

An XYZ Senior officer is the assigned as the Whistle-Blowing Officer. S/he keeps a confidential record of all concerns raised and the outcomes without revealing any specific details, except in cases where allegations of fraud or bribery and corruption are found to be substantiated.

WHAT IF A CONCERN INVOLVES THE WHISTLE BLOWING OFFICER?

If a concern involves the assigned Whistle-Blowing Officer, or if the whistleblower thinks this officer may be biased, the matter should be referred directly to the XYZ Team Leader, but please note that the onus is on the whistleblower first, to provide justification on why s/he believes the matter should come to the XYZ Team Leader at that point.

If a concern involves the XYZ Team Leader, it should be referred directly to the XXXXXXXXX. But please note again that the onus is on the whistleblower to provide justification on why s/he believes the matter should come to the XXXXXXXXX at that point

HOW TO TAKE A MATTER FURTHER

We hope whistleblowers will be satisfied with any action we take, first and foremost. If you're not, and you want to take the matter outside of XYZ, you could contact:

- Our head Office (if this applies)
- Our external auditor;
- The Donor's office in-country
- The Local Charity Registration body
- The police.

FEEDBACK FROM THE WHISTLE-BLOWER

While the main purpose of the policy is to enable XYZ to investigate concerns raised under this policy and take appropriate steps to deal with it, due consideration will be given to the personal support needs of the whistle-blower. In the spirit of developing a learning culture, at the conclusion of the investigation, the whistle-blower may be asked for their opinion on how well they feel that their concern was handled. The whistle-blower will be given as much feedback as is appropriate during the process and in respect of the outcome, in so far as this does not infringe on any duty of confidence.

DECIDING WHETHER TO RAISE A CONCERN

There are common feelings or experiences that can be barriers to raising a concern. Sometimes concerns are not raised because it feels it is none of one's business; it is only a suspicion without hard evidence; it is being disloyal to colleagues, managers or XYZ; it didn't go according to plan when it was raised previously, or other people had a poor experience of whistle-blowing.

It is important, however, for a potential whistle-blower to be clear about the limits of their responsibility and to remember that a whistle-blower is a **witness**, not a complainant. The role of the whistle-blower is to let the facts speak for themselves and to allow the responsible Whistle Blowing Officer to determine what action to take. XYZ would prefer staff and other XYZ stakeholders to raise matters sooner rather than waiting for proof. XYZ appreciates that it may be difficult to decide whether or not to raise a concern, for this reason staff are asked to consider the implications of <u>not</u> blowing the whistle.

CONCLUSION

XYZ is committed to setting and maintaining high standards and a culture of openness, with core values of fairness and trust. This strategy fully supports XYZ's desire to maintain an operating environment, which is free from fraud, theft, bribery and corruption. We have in place a network of systems and procedures to prevent fraud, theft and bribery and corruption and also to assist in dealing with them if they occur. We are determined that these arrangements will keep pace with any future developments in both preventative and detection techniques regarding fraudulent or corrupt activity that may affect our operations in South Sudan.

XYZ will maintain a continuous review of all these systems and procedures. This policy will be reviewed on a regular basis, with a maximum of three years between each review.

8.

BUDGET MONITORING GUIDELINE
FOR PROJECTS

1. INTRODUCTION

Monitoring a project's budget is equally as important as monitoring its technical deliverables. Monitoring a project's budget as well as its technical component, acts as a check on both components, as they both must necessarily tell the same story about the progress of the project. Beyond that, a project's budget embodies the financial agreement between a donor and a grantee – monitoring it reasonably means safeguarding that financial understanding between donor and grantee. Finally, the monitoring process affords the grantee an opportunity to continuously plan ahead; this is done by extrapolating the causes of all current budget behaviours, trying to understand the impacts on the remaining project operations and, preparing to deal with them.

2. HOW TO USE THIS QUESTIONNAIRE

It may be useful to read over this guideline a few times, initially to gain some familiarity, after which some of the processes it suggests will be at the fore of your thinking when you start an actual budget monitoring process. It is equally useful if applied on a line by line basis or used as a reference on subsequent occasions. It may not cover 100% of budget monitoring scenarios, but it will steer the user's monitoring process along areas of core importance.

#	ISSUES TO CONSIDER IN BUDGET MONITORING
	Timing Considerations
1	Although activities are not always going to be executed linearly, it is very useful to compare the percentage of total budget spent to date; with the percentage of the project duration already elapsed. So for example if a 5 year project has just ended its 4th year, we would say the project has travelled 70% of its timeline. If by comparison, the project's total actual expenditure to date is only 30% of its original budget, we should be concerned; and so too, if the overall expenditure to date was 99% and yet the project still had one more full year (or say 20% lifetime) to run. This is used to gauge the "**Pace vs Spend**" of the project and to find out reasons why the balance is not right.

2	A similar comparison can be made between the time elapsed to date (*i.e. project life spent so far ÷ total project life x 100%*) and percentage spending (*i.e. expenditure to date ÷ original budget x 100%*) to date on individual budget lines but with a different consideration. There are some expenditures and activities that have to happen at certain times or within certain periods for the project delivery to be successful. One of the questions to be asking about each budget line, during this monitoring process is this: ***"is this the right time for this activity to be happening?"*** (*Assuming expenditure has been made on that budget line*) or ***"why hasn't this happened yet?"*** (*Assuming no or very low expenditure has been made on that budget line*). It is worth bearing in mind that some budget items like Fixed Assets are normally fully spent in the first years of the project whereas activities such as Final External Evaluations will be left to the last year of implementation. Yet still, others like staff costs, barring any hitches, are normally linear, throughout the life of the project.
3	Usually, donors are reluctant making major budget changes in the very early stages of a contract (*when they haven't had time to see it at work*) or very late in the project life (*when the focus will be on outcomes and minimal disruption*). Once implementation starts, actual expenditures tend to be different from budgeted projections. These 2 in mind, and with knowledge of project time that has elapsed so far, 2 questions are worth asking (i) is this the right time to consider a major budget revision? (*i.e. is this a more likely time for donors to warm up to a budget revision?*) And (ii) Have actual expenditures deviated enough from original forecast to warrant the need for a budget revision?
	Other Reports
4	It is quite important to recognize that a budget monitoring process doesn't only involve, looking at the budget. It is essential to also look at the narrative (*or technical*) reports in order to get a fuller and assured perspective. In that regard, one excellent budget monitoring question to explore is: Are the variances shown in the budget analysis and its explanations, consistent with the contents of the corresponding narrative reports? For Example – *one should be concerned to see a budget line for "Community Trainings" about 40% overspent for the period whereas the narrative report indicates that only a small proportion of the local volunteers could be trained in period because of the onset of the harvest season.*

5	Other reports that could corroborate the variances crystallizing out of the budget monitoring process could be: • Statutory Audit Reports • Reports from other Donors • Evaluation Report • Internal Audit/systems review Reports • Media mentions of the project It is appreciated that not all these reports will be available or accessible during a Budget monitoring process. The point however is, if any is available, it may just be a very useful tool, to cement or contradict the stories portrayed by the budget variances.
	Donor Considerations
6	During a project's Budget Monitoring process, there are a few things that, should they crystallize, are worth highlighting to donors immediately. It is mentioned here so that one can keep an eye out for them throughout the budget monitoring process. Some of these special findings are: (1) Funding, contractually allocated to the period under review *(say, a year)* is likely to remain unspent and/or grantee wishes to have the balance transferred into the following year OR the estimated spending is likely to go over the amount contractually allocated to the period; (2) New activities/new budget lines previously not anticipated, have become necessary and needing a permanent inclusion in the project budget; (3) Political, Operational, Natural, Social, Economic and even Technological events that necessitate the alteration of the project's original focus, and/or fund distributions between budget lines; (4) Changes in core personnel on the project *(and the likely implications, for re-recruitment, interim back-stoppers etc.)*; (5) Financial misappropriations or breaches of any and all kinds; (6) Local Partner changes and the likely financial risks associated with new partnerships.

	Linked Budget Items
7	In budget monitoring, one also needs to consider whether different budget lines, linked directly or indirectly are behaving consistently as they should. Usually, where there are no consistent behaviours, then chances are that either the linkages between these different budget lines are faulty, or the budget line on which an over or underspend has been reported is worth taking a second critical look at. In other words, it is possible for a different budget line, to corroborate the story being told by the variances on another budget line. For example – *where for the first three quarters of the year, an ethnic unrest, has broken out in one of the towns to be covered by the project, then, apart from a huge reduction in the "training of volunteers" budget line for that town, you should also expect a consistent reduction in other budget lines such as local travel within and international travel into that town, per diems related to that work, follow-up meetings scheduled to happen subsequently, graduation ceremonies etc.*
8	More often than not, a budget line variation may arise as a result of a country specific cause. The most popular of these countrywide causes are: inflation, fuel price hikes, new government legislation and exchange rate fluctuations. Where this is the case, it should normally be expected that all project costs *(other than staff costs)*, directly incurred in that country should behave consistently. It should also NOT be expected that such variations in local costs, should affect budget lines related to the project's Headquarters *(assuming it is in a different country)*. For example, *it is questionable to have on overspend on "meeting room hire" explained as resulting from inflationary rises or exchange rate fluctuations and yet no similar variations whatsoever is observed on another in-country budget line such as "project vehicle running costs" or "feeding of participants"*
	Other General Considerations
9	Where a project is being co-financed, check to see, that the amount spent from co-financing source(s) to date, is in the right proportion to donor's contribution for that period. Where the co-finance spending is less than the contractual proportion, one needs to establish, whether this deficit will be made for in subsequent periods. Are there secured funds to cover these deficits? If not, what is likely to be the donor's reaction if reported on? It needs to be borne in mind that most donors, when they require a project to be co-financed, do so with the understanding their funding risk exposure is equal to their proportion in the funding mix. As such, when agreed co-financing contributions fall less than agreed, donor funding risk is disproportionately increased automatically.

10	Read through the variance notes provided for each budget line variance (*i.e. the difference between budgeted amounts and actual expenditures*) and consider whether the explanations provided for over/under expenditures are in line with the "Project Context": "context" means, your own knowledge (*and all available open information*) about the political, operational, economic, social and technological environment in which the project is situated. E.g. of Social and political context - *a budget line for "community meetings" goes above budget by 30% for meetings held between Thursday and Sunday of the last month in the 2nd quarter: However, your social context knowledge assures you that, the particular community doesn't come out on Fridays because it is their holyday and that the Saturday in question was the same date local elections were being held* – that should make you question the validity and reasonableness of the overspend.
11	Are expenditures broadly in line with budgets? (*up to 10% deviation from budget is considered normal*)? Is grant income received, broadly in line with the budgeted total expenditure for that period? Consider also whether or not the variances being observed are temporary or permanent. If permanent, what are the implications for funding in subsequent years (*if the project hasn't yet completed its full term*)
12	Have there been any significantly large expenditure variances (*positive or negative*) occurring and what have been their causes? The causes, (*whatever they are*) need to be classified as one of the 3 below in order to help categorize their treatment: (1) ***Generally a causative factor within Budget holder's control:*** *with this, Budget holder should consider what changes can be made to the causative factor, to re-align the deviating expenditures to original positions; it should also be considered whether the deviated position is the new correct position and therefore to make it the new default – and if so, how that affects the budgets of subsequent years;* (2) ***The causative factor is entirely outside of Budget Holder's (BH) control:*** *here, consideration needs to be given to what the BH can do, to mitigate the effects of a recurrence of this event on budget deviation. If however the resulting budget deviation has turned out to be value-adding, then the BH needs to consider first, whether this welcome deviation needs to be sustained throughout the project's life; then, what can be put in place to take advantage of the unplanned occurrence, should it recur;* (3) ***Entirely new activities that have arisen as a result of the project's evolution:*** *Is (are) the new activity reasonable? Is it adding value to the project? Can it be justified to the donor? Will it suffice only for this period or does it have to form a permanent part of the rest of the project's life and if so, how will it be funded if the donor is not likely to provide additional funding beyond what has already been contracted?*

3. GENERIC SUGGESTIONS FOR BUDGET VARIATIONS

Listed below, a few generic solutions budget-holders can consider, in dealing with budget variations:

1. Consider the possibility of using permanent under-spends to fund permanent over-spends? Be careful however, about conditions that donors may have placed on the use of grant funds – some donors may not allow you to make such changes once a budget is agreed;

2. Do the budget titles still accurately describe the activities on the ground? And do the amounts allocated to each budget-line still appear reasonable? It might be a good time to review and rework the project budget in liaison with the donor and all related stakeholders;

3. Consider the possibility of controlling the causes of over-spends or their impacts in future months? Note that some costs are fixed and so cannot be controlled – in this case, aim to put structures in place that will reduce their impact when they occur;

4. Where the need for new activities, or an increased expenditure on already planned activities become necessary, consider the possibility of finding and getting additional funding from same or other donors, or even approaching your senior officers to consider using unrestricted or other designated reserves;

5. In some circumstances, the variances arising can be corrected by: aligning the timing either individually, of fund receipts and activity implementations (expenditure), or between them. E.g. maybe some expenses can be delayed, and others procured early.

Whatever lines of action are decided on, the budget-holder must ensure core stakeholders such as donors, local partner and other participating organisations, that may be affected by the change are consulted.

ABOUT THE AUTHOR

Marricke Kofi Gane (*Formerly Charles Kofi Fekpe*) has a total of 12 years working experience, 8 of which has been in International Development and Aid Effectiveness, with specializations in grant management, financial capability due diligence, financial system reviews, overseas office set-ups, auditing, risk management, training, donor compliance, contracting and overseas field operations.

In that time, he successfully managed at least 13 funds or grants for International Aid Agencies as well as major Government and Private Donor institutions, with values ranging from as low as £15 million to £150 million per individual fund or grant.

He is a Ghanaian-British, married with 3 children and currently resident in the United Kingdom.

SEE MORE OF HIS PROFESSIONAL EXPERTISE AT

www.grants-consultant.com

AUTHOR'S OTHER WORKS

Title: Is This Why Africa Is? (E-book & Paperback)

Description: I ask all the questions about Africa that nobody else will. Deep, profound questions

Availability: Amazon & Kindle

Link to View: http://goo.gl/ecRMig

Title: Where Did God Hide His Diamonds? (E-book & Paperback)

Description: Discovering what exactly God has hidden in you, finding it & prospering freely from it

Availability: Amazon & Kindle

Link to View: http://goo.gl/ecRMig

Title: Doing Business with God (E-book & Paperback)

Description: 60 shocking biblical principles for extraordinary leadership, business and politics.

Availability: Amazon & Kindle

Link to View: http://goo.gl/ecRMig

Title: Midnight Philosophies (E-book & Paperback)

Description: My Deep thoughts, Philosophies, Reflections – Whispers of my mind.

Availability: Amazon & Kindle

Link to View: http://goo.gl/ecRMig

Title: This Godly Child of Mine (E-book & Paperback)

Description: A revelatory book on how to raise godly children in a perverse and lawless world

Availability: Amazon & Kindle

Link to View: http://goo.gl/ecRMig

Title: The Deputy Minister for Corruption (E-book & Paperback)

Description: A Novel

Availability: Amazon & Kindle

Link to View: http://goo.gl/ecRMig

Title:	A Dove in the Storm (E-book & Paperback)
Description:	A Novel
Availability:	Amazon & Kindle
Link to View:	http://goo.gl/ecRMig

Title:	100% JOB INTERVIEW SUCCESS (E-book & Paperback)
Description:	A simple, straightforward guide to passing every job interview you attend.
Availability:	Amazon & Kindle
Link to View:	http://goo.gl/ecRMig

Title:	Bible-by-Heart (Mobile App)
Description:	A simple but effective App to help anyone memorize 500 Bible verses in a year.
Availability:	iTunes & Google Play Stores
Link to View:	http://goo.gl/T3UdPN (i-Tunes)
Link to View:	http://goo.gl/ljnECR (Android)

Title:	Holy Rat (Mobile Game)
Description:	An exciting Christian mobile game that unwittingly gets you addicted to the word.
Availability:	iTunes & Google Play Stores
Link to View:	http://goo.gl/bygjBi (i-Tunes)
Link to View:	http://goo.gl/F18RM0 (Android)

Made in the USA
Middletown, DE
01 November 2015